my children in Heaven

A Story of Grief, Hope, and Love

ROSEANNE M. COLLISON

My Children in Heaven: A Story of Grief, Hope, and Love
Published by Final Piece Publishing
Denver, CO

All Bible verses, except where otherwise noted, are taken from:

THE HOLY BIBLE, NEW INTERNATIONAL VERSION®, NIV®
Copyright © 1973, 1978, 1984, 2011 by Biblica, Inc.® Used by permission. All rights reserved worldwide.

Bible verses marked [WEB] are taken from the World English Bible.

Scripture quotations marked [RSV] are from the Revised Standard Version of the Bible, copyright © 1946, 1952, and 1971 the Division of Christian Education of the National Council of the Churches of Christ in the United States of America. Used by permission. All rights reserved.

ISBN: 978-0-578-78083-2
Christian Living / Personal Memoirs
Cover and Interior design by Victoria Wolf,
wolfdesignandmarketing.com
Cover artwork painted by Mark Egbert

To my precious Daniel, Sarah, Michael, and Jesse.
I will see you in heaven …

Contents

"There is nothing that can replace the absence of someone dear to us, and one should not even attempt to do so. One must simply hold out and endure it. At first that sounds very hard, but at the same time it is also a great comfort. For to the extent the emptiness truly remains unfilled one remains connected to the other person through it. It is wrong to say that God fills the emptiness. God in no way fills it but much more leaves it precisely unfilled and thus helps us preserve—even in pain—the authentic relationship. Furthermore, the more beautiful and full the remembrances, the more difficult the separation. But gratitude transforms the torment of memory into silent joy. One bears what was lovely in the past not as a thorn but as a precious gift deep within, a hidden treasure of which one can always be certain."

—Dietrich Bonhoeffer

Acknowledgments

I WOULD LIKE TO EXPRESS my gratitude to our wonderful family members, friends, and professionals who supported Brian, Constance, and me during this difficult season in our life. "Carry each other's burdens, and in this way you will fulfill the law of Christ" (Galatians 6:2). We would not have been able to make it if it weren't for those who lovingly carried us through it.

Thank you to our parents, Marge and Paul Bezdek, Lynn Watson, Mike and Kim Collison, Mark Egbert, and our siblings, Greg and Amanda Collison, Luke Egbert, and Neil Bezdek for your unending love and support.

Thank you to our current and past church family, especially Pastor Joe Warring, Mike and Tina Cohenour, Jennifer and Chris Sterling, Kelli and Brady Hustad, Melissa and Geoff Armstrong, Mac and Julie Perry, and Ginger Popp.

I am forever indebted to Charlotte Dragon and her family for unconditionally loving all of us but especially Constance. Thank you to Jane and James Hutcheson for your continual prayers.

I am humbled by the overwhelming support and empathy from Laura Huene and *String of Pearls*. Thank you for the wonderful care that I received from the nurses at *Presbyterian St. Luke's Hospital* Neonatal Unit, especially Julie Rael, RN.

I am grateful for the compassionate care that I received from Jacqueline Ziernicki, MD. I also thank Rachel Norwood, MD, and Kim Wise, LPC, for their insight and counseling.

I want to acknowledge the other mothers of loss, especially Jenny Glowacki. I am grateful for our long runs, honest conversations, and fresh coffee. I also appreciate the friendships I have made with Willow, Janelle, Astrid, and other grieving mothers who I frequently meet. You are not alone in remembering your babies.

And most importantly, Brian, thank you for your support, patience, understanding, and love. I am blessed to be married to the best husband there is. I would not want to be on this journey with anyone but you!

Prologue

MY HUSBAND AND I sat in the exam room, waiting for the doctor to come in and discuss the results of our ultrasound. Here we were again for the third time in two years. My last two pregnancies ended in miscarriages, and I so desperately wanted another baby. I had a sinking feeling that we were about to receive bad news again. "Everything will be okay," said Brian, trying to reassure me.

The young OB-GYN nervously entered the room with the ultrasound images in her hand. I didn't need to hear her words; I could tell she was about to confirm my suspicion. She started to explain that the ultrasound revealed some serious abnormalities. Immediately my thoughts went to having yet another miscarriage. *Three in a row? How could that be?* As we tried to absorb the bad news, little did we know what the future held for the baby I was carrying, or that I would be strong enough to get through the hardest experience of my life.

CHAPTER ONE

The Beginning

BRIAN AND ROSEANNE

I live in a very boring suburb. It is safe, clean, and close to the grocery store. My husband, Brian, and I live in a nice house in an average neighborhood with lots of stop signs and houses that all look the same—cookie cutter suburbia at its finest. We have a great church community and live ten minutes from my parents and my husband's mom. We are very blessed.

If I could craft my life the way I dreamt about it when I was young and unattached, I would live somewhere exotic or at least charming and preferably by the beach. I would work, marry young, and have two or three children on a timeline that I would be fully in control of and then be a stay-at-home mom with no financial challenges.

Sounds nice, doesn't it? But life doesn't happen the way we envision, and God has bigger, more interesting plans than we can imagine. I never considered the challenges that we would face in fertility and childbirth or that having multiple children might not even be a possibility for us. But then again, I am grateful that I didn't know the storm we were about to enter. God, in His wisdom, doesn't allow us to see the future. If He had pulled the curtain back, I never would have had the courage to venture through it.

Brian and I met in high school but didn't date. We reconnected years later when I ran into him at a bar in downtown Denver. After he strategically used my dad as a loan officer when buying his first house, my parents told me they thought he would make a good husband for me. It took a few years of me getting past his poor fashion sense (such as jeans purchased from truck stops) to see what my parents and my best friends saw. God's plan is perfect, and I couldn't be married to a better man. Our daughter, Constance, is six and the absolute joy of our life. She is kind, smart, and precocious.

I grew up going to church, and my faith became my own in high school. Brian went to church when he was young, fell away from his faith in high school and college, but came back to it through his mom and some friends after college.

Years ago, I remember being part of a women's Bible study on the book of Revelation. In talking about being reunited with loved ones in heaven, someone mentioned the story of a former church member who had been pregnant but found out that the baby had a terminal neurological birth defect. The baby's condition allowed him to live and fully develop inside the womb, but he would be brain dead once he was born. The mother chose to carry the baby and enjoy the precious time she had with him in the womb before he was born and died.

I remember being absolutely horrified by the story. I couldn't think of too many things worse than carrying a baby that you knew would die. *I could never imagine going through something so terrible.* Little did I know how my story would unfold a few years later ...

CONSTANCE

It took about a year and a half to get pregnant with Constance. At the time, that was hard for us. Each month brought a fresh disappointment and a new argument with Brian as to what to do about not conceiving. Brian wanted to trust God and give it time. I wanted to see the doctor and use what God had taught humankind about medicine to get some answers.

Our conflict came to a head on a scenic hike over Labor Day weekend in 2010. We were camping with friends at Golden Gate Canyon State Park west of Denver, and we broke off by ourselves for an afternoon hike. I brought up our struggle to get pregnant, and it quickly escalated into a good old marital fight. We took turns shouting into the back of each other's heads for about six hours on a scenic, narrow trail under the glowing aspen leaves. We stopped arguing if another hiker passed us but started up again even while they were still within earshot. We did not come to a resolution that day, but we conceived about two weeks later—effectively ending our argument. About eight months later, we found ourselves holding a beautiful five-pound baby girl!

Constance was born at thirty-five and a half weeks. Going into labor so early was a total shock—I had not even packed my "go bag." As we frantically ran around the house in the middle of the night, we were like actors straight out of a movie scene, trying to think of what we needed to take with us and stopping every five minutes for a contraction. We had not even decided on a hospital yet. We threw the car seat—still in the box—into the trunk of my car and took the toll road to a hospital at 5:00 a.m. on a Sunday morning. *You know, to avoid the traffic.*

Needless to say, even if Constance did cook for the full nine months, I do not think I would have been prepared for motherhood. I think I am a good mom, but I had not cared for an infant since my babysitting years, and I didn't remember a thing! I wanted to breastfeed, but I was more than a little surprised when I found out after delivery that this new creature had to eat every three hours *around the clock* and that feeding can take up to an hour. *When was I supposed to sleep!?*

We brought Constance home via the toll road on a Tuesday afternoon—*again, to avoid traffic.* We laid her in her bassinet and checked on her often to assure ourselves that she was breathing, terrified of the responsibility that was now before us. It was a very stressful first few nights. I wanted to do a good job, so naturally I watched videos on YouTube about the proper way to change a diaper. When the nurse called to follow up once we were home, I asked, "How many hours a day am I supposed to hold the baby?" as if there were a prescribed daily amount. She laughed and said, "As much as possible!"

Regardless of our lack of experience, we survived and so did Constance. She grew quickly and went from being a premature, colicky infant to a lovely chunk of a baby within a few months. We were now parents and excited to have started a little family of our own.

CHAPTER TWO

Daniel

AFTER A COUPLE YEARS ADJUSTING to being a family of three, we were ready to try again. I hoped it wouldn't take as long to get pregnant and, sure enough, it only took a few months. We must have gotten out all the kinks for how to conceive during the year-and-a-half trial with Constance. In January 2013, we took a pregnancy test and went out to celebrate the good news with an Italian dinner and a trip to see the Van Gogh exhibit at the Denver Art Museum. We toasted our water glasses to the excitement that we would become a family of four the following September. This was the expected progression in our life, and we couldn't have been happier.

We were part of a medical co-op at the time, and I wanted to minimize medical expenses. While we would be reimbursed for costs associated with pregnancy and delivery, we would have to first pay for the bills upfront, which makes one more mindful of the cost. By my calculation, I was about five weeks along. I went to a Christian pregnancy center for our first ultrasound. Brian and Constance came too. I filled out a form, and we waited to be called back to the ultrasound room.

Once there, we looked at the grainy screen with the ultrasound tech as she searched for a life. She said she couldn't see a fetal pole or a heartbeat, but it was early so we should come back in three weeks. I agreed to the recommendation but left filled with worry. I had a few of the classic signs of pregnancy, but they were very mild. With Constance, I had every symptom one could read about. I threw up at least daily until about fourteen weeks and weekly after that. I read that each pregnancy is different, so I tried not to fret over the lack of symptoms.

My mother-in-law, Lynn, went with me to the second ultrasound appointment at eight weeks. Brian was traveling for a new job, and I didn't want to wait for him to get back into town. I was eager for confirmation that everything was going to be okay. But again, the ultrasound tech couldn't quite see what she was looking for. She saw some fetal movement, but couldn't get a good heartbeat. She recommended going to my OB-GYN because they had better machines. I cried for the first time in the ultrasound room. Lynn gave me a hug. As I look back now, that was the beginning of three years of suffering. I would have about fifteen more ultrasounds over the next few years for four different pregnancies—all of them indicating bad news.

I immediately made a doctor's appointment for as soon as they could get me in. It was January 31. Brian and I nervously sat in the waiting room. Our appointment started with an ultrasound. The ultrasound machine at my OB-GYN's office was more sophisticated than the free one at the pregnancy center. This time, we were able to see a little fetus with a heartbeat. *Praise the Lord! What a relief!* The yolk sac, however, was enlarged, and the size of the fetus wasn't matching up with the date of my last period. Similar to the appointment at the pregnancy clinic, we were asked to come back in three weeks. I would be about eleven weeks by my math, but eight weeks by theirs. The tech said, "Perhaps your dates are off." We were sent home, again, and told not to worry. I would hear that a lot in the next few years. For the record, none of my dates were off. I know how it all works.

Our next appointment was February 19. Brian was on the road again, so I asked my friend, Alicia, to come with me. I drove to the appointment alone and met Alicia there. She offered to pick me up, but we live on opposite sides of town, and the OB-GYN office was somewhat in the middle. We had another ultrasound, and this time there was no heartbeat. The fetus was measuring about the same. Holding back tears, I dressed and went into the exam room to wait for my doctor.

I switched doctors after having Constance. We nicknamed that one Dr. Scary. She was very intelligent and direct but seemed irked when we called her at midnight around thirty-five weeks to tell her that I was in labor with Constance. She didn't like the hospital that we chose, even though we were given it as an option by our clinic, and she had privileges there. My new OB-GYN, Dr. Ziernicki, was at the same practice.

She had a much kinder demeanor and, in hindsight, she was a much better doctor for us, given all the heartbreak that was on the horizon.

It was only my second or third time meeting Dr. Ziernicki, and she was very compassionate. She told me that first-trimester miscarriages are common and can happen for a number of reasons—sometimes known and sometimes not. Some women do not even realize they are pregnant. *Who the heck are those women?!* She gave me a hug and said 25 percent of pregnancies end in miscarriage. *Great, I am a statistic. Is that somehow supposed to be reassuring?* I had not had any bleeding yet, but I was told that, one way or another, the fetal tissue had to be expelled.

"Can't the body just absorb everything back?" I asked. *Like hitting a big undo button?* The answer was no. There was a newly formed baby inside of me, no longer developing, that had to come out.

My options were to wait for a few weeks to see if I could miscarry naturally, take some pills at home to get the bleeding started, or have a D&C procedure. I didn't even know how to spell D&C, but it didn't sound like fun. *DNC? Like the Democratic National Committee?* Dr. Ziernicki explained she would open the cervix and use suction to remove the birth tissue from my uterus. *Yuck and no thanks.* But I also did not want to wait for what felt like a bloody bomb to explode in potentially an inconvenient or embarrassing place, so I opted to take the medication. While all the options sounded awful, I liked the idea of being in the comfort and privacy of my home.

Dr. Ziernicki prescribed a drug called Cytotec—to be inserted vaginally—and Vicodin. She also told me to take the next week off of work. I asked, "Would I really feel that bad physically?" She said no, but to heal emotionally. I thought to myself, *Why would I need to do that?*

My birthday, February 21, was two days later. We celebrated the best we could, and I hoped that next year would be better. Brian was still out of town, so I went out to dinner with my parents and Constance, who was two and a half at the time. She was particularly a handful that night, but I got through it by acting happy on the outside despite feeling alone and sad that there was a dead baby in my belly. Surely my next birthday would be better. Brian came home the next day.

I took the pills Saturday morning and then the wait began. The unpleasantness of inserting the pills vaginally embodied what an all-around horrible experience a miscarriage is. Dr. Ziernicki said it would take about four hours or so for the medication to kick in. I laid around until that afternoon when the cramping started. Brian was out running errands. Doubled over in pain, barely able to utter a complete sentence, I called him to come home. For some reason, I did not want to take the Vicodin before I had pain. In retrospect, that was dumb. Of course I should have. I took the medicine as soon as the pain hit, but the cramping ratcheted up to "severe" very quickly. Brian came home, held my hand as I cried, and we watched *The Office*, my favorite show that year, as a way to pass the time.

I bled heavily for the next twelve hours or so. My parents took Constance for the night, and Lynn, Brian's mom, came over for pizza and games. It was nice to have a distraction for such an awful and, frankly, disgusting event. I passed the fetal tissue that evening, and I examined the small whitish mass on the toilet paper. I wept and flushed it down the toilet. The next day, I woke up with a broken heart. *Yesterday I was pregnant and today I am not.* It was the worst feeling I had ever experienced.

I am ashamed to admit that, prior to this, I thought people were merely sad about miscarriages because they were disappointed that they were not going to have a baby. This miscarriage was my first real experience with grief and loss—and I handled it very poorly. I did not think it was a significant loss that deserved to be acknowledged and processed. I told my boss and took Monday off from work but returned on Tuesday as if nothing had happened. I did not give my heart room to grieve. I tried to carry on with business as usual—working, being a mom and a wife. I was exhausted physically and emotionally but did not allow myself to rest. The problem was that a significant loss *had* occurred. I was heartbroken, and while I mentally tried to deny it existed, the grief found other ways to emerge.

Dr. Ziernicki asked me to return two weeks later for a follow-up ultrasound to see if all the pregnancy material had come out. I was ushered back into the ultrasound room. At least this time, I was not hoping for a heartbeat. There was still some tissue left, so she gave me the option of trying the Cytotec again at home or doing a D&C. Seeing as though neither option was appealing, I asked if maybe we could just opt to do nothing.

She said the tissue could get infected, and I could wind up in the hospital in septic shock. *Okay, message received. It won't just go away if I ignore it.* If only I knew that was true for my grief too. I did not want to repeat the home experience, so having a D&C was my choice by process of elimination.

My doctor's office was pretty high-tech, so they were able to do the D&C on-site, rather than have me go to the hospital. The procedure was scheduled for a Friday afternoon in March. I was so sad to have the procedure, but I also wanted this miscarriage experience, which was now going on three weeks, to be over. Not surprisingly, I went to work that day as if it were no big deal. Brian met me at the doctor's office. This appointment felt different than a normal one. I looked at the other women in the waiting room. Some had big bellies. Some were older women. Did anyone realize we were waiting to do something awful, traumatic, unpleasant?

I was called back to an area that I had not been to before. I met a whole bunch of medical people who were not usually at the clinic, like the anesthesiology nurse. She was a stout, older nurse who reminded me of my Aunt Kathie, who was also a nurse and, coincidentally, had once worked at Planned Parenthood, to the horror of my mom's Catholic family. Aunt Kathie is kind and loving, just like the nurse that day. I found comfort in the resemblance.

They gave me an IV and some medications to start the numbing and sedation. Then I was taken to the surgical room and had to say goodbye to Brian. The room was cold, but they had hand-knit blankets, which was comforting. Since the procedure was done in-house, I was kept awake and given, frankly, some pretty great drugs.

Then the suction began. It was awful. I looked at the ceiling and tried not to think about the sounds coming from below. Finally it was over. I was reunited with Brian, who gave me a hug. The nurse and Brian walked me out to his car when it was over. Brian had a bar of chocolate waiting for me in the car, but I was too woozy to eat it. It was very sweet of him. He has always been very loving and caring, but looking back, we were such novices at experiencing adversity together.

Dr. Ziernicki gave us the option to have the tissue tested for genetic problems, but we did not want to pay for anything extra and figured this would be a one-time thing—a blip in our attempt to grow our family. In hindsight, I wish I had done all possible testing after each loss. It may have guided our choices in the future and even prevented some future heartache. Yet at the same time, this has been our experience, and it certainly has been a rich one. Would I change how we handled it? *Yes.* Do I regret how we handled it? *Hard to say.* Nobody wants to face loss and suffering, but one gains so much through the trial.

Brian drove me home around four o'clock and put me to bed. I got up around eight o'clock in the evening to use the bathroom and slept straight through until the next morning. I remained in bed that day and took it easy the rest of the weekend. I took Monday and Tuesday off, but after that, it was back to work. Physically, I was healing, but emotionally I was raw. The grief was wearing me down. I didn't take the time I needed to let my heart heal. A few weeks later, I wound up getting the worst cold I ever had. Not only did it land me in bed for a full week, but I got double pinkeye—not a pretty sight.

The week of rest was necessary and good for me. I took time to pray and grieve. I was able to start working through my grief and had some good quiet times praying and journaling. I was reading the book of Daniel in the Old Testament at the time. During one of my sessions, I read:

"In my vision at night I looked, and there before me was one like a son of man, coming with the clouds of heaven. He approached the Ancient of Days and was led into his presence. He was given authority, glory and sovereign power; all nations and peoples of every language worshiped him. His dominion is an everlasting dominion that will not pass away, and his kingdom is one that will never be destroyed" (Daniel 7:13–14).

The words jumped out at me. I was struck by the power and glory of Jesus returning to earth. Jesus is my hope and, even when there is such great loss in this fallen world, we have eternal hope in God's promises. We will see Jesus, and He will restore this world. I felt in my heart that this baby was going to be a boy, so we named him Daniel.

A few years prior to this, I had read the book *Heaven is for Real* by Todd Burpo and Lynn Vincent in which a little boy explains what heaven is like after a near-death experience. He said he saw a baby in heaven that was his sister. His mom had miscarried a baby, but the parents never told him about it. He said the baby didn't have a name since his mom never named it. What a gift from God—we get to name our children and their names will follow them to heaven. I found incredible comfort in thinking that my miscarried baby had a soul, and I will get to meet him someday.

Psalm 139:13–16 says:

"For you created my inmost being; you knit me together in my mother's womb. I praise you because I am fearfully and wonderfully made; your works are wonderful, I know that full well. My frame was not hidden from you when I was made in the secret place, when I was woven together in the depths of the earth. Your eyes saw my unformed body."

God is the creator of life, and our souls certainly exist in the womb, even before life is possible. I felt that Daniel was a boy, but if I find out Daniel is really a Danielle when I get to heaven, that will be okay too.

Even after the rest, I was still struggling. I started having anxiety and some depression that spring. One morning, while reading the newspaper at breakfast, I saw there was a cat show competition in town. I have always been a cat person (*controversial to admit, I know*). We already had two cats, Stormy and Stray Cat Strut. Before having Constance, I would carry Stormy around the house like a baby. Within about two minutes of bringing Constance home, Stormy was demoted to Cat.

On a whim, we went to the cat show just to look at the pretty cats and their fanatic owners. Brian befriended an older couple who had a retired champion purebred named Suntaj Sugar Magnolia, or "Maggie" for short. Before we knew it, we had brought home an eighteen-pound behemoth of a long-hair Maine Coon. She was my miscarriage cat. And although it wasn't a baby, it helped.

The anxiety persisted, however, and I just felt "off." In June, I finally went to a counselor whom I had seen before. She was a great counselor to talk to about marriage, self-esteem, and identity issues like I had previously, but she did not specialize in grief work. We were able at least to talk about my anxiety and how grieving made it hard for me to live up to my standards in other areas, like work, but I did not feel like we directly addressed the loss which I carried with me in the months to come.

CHAPTER THREE

Sarah

WE GOT THROUGH THE SUMMER. We still wanted a baby, of course. Dr. Ziernicki did not think we had anything to worry about, but she told us to wait three menstrual cycles before trying again. Once I felt we were in the clear, we had some marital fun and got pregnant within a couple of months. My period was a few days late, and we were about to go camping for a weekend in August at Rocky Mountain National Park. I took a pregnancy test right before we left, which turned out to be positive. I brought the test to show Brian immediately. We hugged and I cried. Fear sunk in almost immediately. Our miscarriage with Daniel was so hard. This was what we wanted, but what if we miscarried again?

It was nice to escape town and have time away to think about what we were getting ourselves into. We went on a five-mile hike Saturday morning, and it was so much harder than it should have been. Even being only five weeks pregnant, I felt so lightheaded and fatigued. I barely made it back to camp a few hours later.

I was terrified of miscarrying again. Similar to the last time, I did not have the strong signs of pregnancy or nausea like I did with Constance. I called Dr. Ziernicki the Monday after camping. We went into her office around six weeks, and I had an ultrasound. My measurements were off—again—and they did not see a heartbeat. They did bloodwork to see if my hCG levels were doubling—a telltale sign of a viable pregnancy—and to check my progesterone level. She told me not to worry, which was as impossible as telling me not to breathe.

My progesterone level came back normal, but my hCG levels were not doubling—not a good sign. We returned to Dr. Ziernicki's office a week later and had another ultrasound. This time, there was a heartbeat! *Praise God!* For both Daniel's pregnancy and this one, getting to see a heartbeat was a tremendous gift from God. *Life.* Although there was a heartbeat, I had an enlarged yolk sac, just like with Daniel. Dr. Ziernicki recommended that we wait and come back in three weeks to compare. Another wait. My heart ached, and I felt a pit in my stomach. I was scared we were going down the same path as we had with Daniel.

By now it was September 2013, and I was nine weeks along. Daniel was supposed to be born in September. We went to see Dr. Ziernicki and had—you guessed it—an ultrasound. Initially I had a little nausea here and there, but I did not feel any signs of pregnancy in the last few weeks. The ultrasound tech fished around, looking for the fetus. She found the yolk sac, which was just as large as before. Attached was the fetal pole, but with no growth and, more importantly, no heartbeat.

I was heartbroken. Another baby had died inside of me. I was given the same three crappy options: use medication to miscarry at home, wait, or have a D&C. The Cytotec was so unpleasant and did not even finish the job last time, making the miscarriage experience drag out. I would have my ten-year college reunion in just three weeks, and did not want the miscarriage time bomb ruining that. So, I opted for another D&C, as awful as it was. I just wanted to get it over with.

This time, though, I felt prepared for it. I knew what to expect and planned to take more time off of work and to allow myself to rest. I understood this time that a miscarriage is a true loss, and I needed to take time to grieve. While my fear came true, I also felt relief in knowing I no longer had to carry that worry with me. Although I wish we had a different outcome, receiving the bad news was better than the intangible dread of the unknown. We went through the same procedure as last time at the doctor's office. They gave me a tampon dipped in something to numb me up and some medicine to start softening the cervix. Next, I got an IV inserted and took some initial pain medication and anti-nausea medication. Brian was able to stay with me for all of this, but then they got me ready to go into the surgical room, and he had to stay in the exam room and wait. I hated being separated and felt alone. That was when the warm blankets were especially comforting.

The D&C procedure seemed to be much shorter this time. Since I was awake, although totally numb and very woozy, I could still feel pressure as she scraped away my uterine lining. I asked Dr. Ziernicki if she was sure she got everything, and she showed me what they sucked out. I also asked to see the fetus, which surprised them. I touched the whitish tissue and said a tearful goodbye. The nurse and Dr. Ziernicki cried a bit with me too. One of the worst parts of a D&C is hearing the suction noise. For days after, I felt like a jack-o'-lantern—carved out and hollow. Brian brought me home again and put me to bed. This time, I slept until about noon the next day.

I knew to take more time off of work. Monday was a recovery day for me physically, and I took Tuesday to pray, journal, and recover emotionally and spiritually. I spent half the day in prayer, journaling and crying, and the other half of the day sleeping and watching lighthearted chick flicks like *Mamma Mia!* and *Sweet Home Alabama*.

I was reading Genesis at the time and specifically the story of Abraham and his wife, Sarah. God promised Abraham that his descendants would be as numerous as the stars in the sky. However, Abraham and Sarah were eighty-five and seventy-five years old, respectively, and without any children. It was painful for Sarah to be barren, not only because of her own desire but also culturally because women were shunned if they could not have children. Knowing God's promise, Sarah took matters into her own hands. Rather than trusting God, Sarah thrust Hagar, her maidservant, onto Abraham to produce a descendant for them. However, once Hagar conceived, Sarah quickly became jealous and mistreated Hagar. Hagar fled to the desert only to be called back to Abraham by God. In His mercy and as part of His divine plan, God still blessed Sarah in her old age with a son, named Isaac, thirteen years after Hagar had her son, Ishmael.

Even after both women had their sons, Sarah was still insecure about Hagar and Ishmael's place in the family. She sent Hagar away into the desert again. Hagar was forced to go into the desert with only the amount of food and water that she could carry, which quickly ran out. In desperation, she left her son under a bush and went a few hundred yards away so she did not have to watch him die. God, in his unending mercy, heard her cry and led them to a well, sparing them from certain death (Genesis 15:1–7, Genesis 16–18, 21:1–21).

I have read that story many times now over the last three years and connect with it in a different way each time. Sometimes passages in the Bible are written matter-of-factly, and one has to draw out the emotions in them, and sometimes the emotions that the characters are feeling just pop off the page. I connect with the emotion expressed by both women. Honestly, I can understand why Sarah thrust Hagar onto Abraham only to mistreat her after she conceived. I feel moved reading about Hagar's fear of dying in the desert and how she must have felt when the Lord said He would provide for her.

I know the pain of Sarah's barrenness and understand how she doubted whether God would give her a child. However, I also laugh out loud when she tried to lie to the angel who called her on it.

"Then the Lord said to Abraham, 'Why did Sarah laugh and say, "Will I really have a child, now that I am old?" Is anything too hard for the Lord? I will return to you at the appointed time next year, and Sarah will have a son.' Sarah was afraid, so she lied and said, 'I did not laugh.' But he said, 'Yes, you did laugh'" (Genesis 18:13–15).

Oopsies Sarah—it never goes well when you try to hide things from God!

As I read Genesis during this pregnancy, I felt my baby was a girl. Who knows, but I just went with my hunch. We named her Sarah. I miss each of our babies in different ways—because they are individual people and each pregnancy was a unique experience. I am pained in thinking about Sarah. For those few weeks that I knew I was pregnant, I did not allow myself to connect with the baby the same way I had with Daniel. Fearful of miscarrying, I wanted to protect my heart from the pain of losing another baby. It made sense, but it did not work. I really just missed out on getting to know her while she was with me, as short as it was. I can't wait to meet her in heaven. I really miss her.

After the D&C procedure, I grieved over the created being whom I didn't get to know. Seeing her heartbeat was a tremendous gift. Like Daniel, Sarah lived, even if it was just for a few short weeks inside my womb. After a day of praying and grieving, I was filled with a tremendous, supernatural sense of hope. I still wanted a baby to hold, and I strongly felt God tell me next time would be different. It was different, although not at all how I envisioned.

The second miscarriage was my easiest loss, which sounds like an oxymoron—easy loss. The first miscarriage, as horrible as it was, prepared me for the second one. I knew what to expect for the procedure and recovery. I gave myself time to heal. By grieving Sarah, I also grieved losing Daniel. In a relatively short amount of time, I felt whole again and back to my normal self, which I never really felt after Daniel.

My ten-year college reunion was just a couple of weeks later. I had gained about eight pounds while pregnant with Daniel, lost it, and then lost about five more pounds while pregnant with Sarah. It was pretty fantastic timing—relative to the reunion—although I would have settled for losing weight from having the flu instead. Despite feeling a little fragile from my loss, it was great to get to enjoy a girls' weekend in Santa Barbara and be able to have a few drinks at our favorite old bars.

While it was fun to reconnect with friends and reminisce about good times, I was struck with the reality that we were fully entrenched in adulthood. We had families and careers. We also all had loss and hardships in our lives. A friend had a chronic illness, another had an abusive mother-in-law, another was now divorced. We knew people who had died.

In college, we were happy-go-lucky barely-adults, and now we had a little bit of reality under our belts. It made us more interesting, stronger people. I returned home and went back to normal life for a few months before we were able to try to conceive once more. After all, I still longed to have another baby.

I had a follow-up appointment with Dr. Ziernicki when I returned home. Brian and I had opted again not to have the fetal tissue tested for genetic problems—we didn't think that we would need this valuable information in the future. Dr. Ziernicki was supportive of our choice because even having two first-trimester miscarriages was common. She tested me for a few autoimmune disorders and checked my thyroid to see if I had a blood clotting disorder. Everything came back normal, and other tests were not necessary since we had had a healthy pregnancy with Constance. She recommended that Brian and I get our karyotypes analyzed to see if we had any underlying chromosomal abnormalities, but we did not think it would be worth the cost. Dr. Ziernicki gave us the go-ahead to try again, but she said that the next time we conceive, she would put me on progesterone and baby aspirin as a precaution as soon as we found out. She gave me a prescription that day to fill for when I would need it next.

Having two miscarriages in a row was heartbreaking. But as I said, I was able to heal from the first one by grieving the second one. And they both still seemed like flukes. Part of the death and decay in our fallen world. My mom had two miscarriages in a row between me and my younger brother. I still wanted a second child and strongly felt that we would have one. 2013 was winding down, and I felt that 2014 certainly would be better! And sure enough, at the end of 2013—December 17 to be exact—we found out we were pregnant again!

CHAPTER FOUR

Michael's Life

PREGNANT AGAIN

I was determined to have a baby. I was filled with hope that our next pregnancy would be different. Brian and I tried to wait three cycles but ended up finding out that we were pregnant at the beginning of December. I was so excited! And so nervous. We had just joined a new medical co-op called Samaritan Ministries that would be a tremendous help for the remainder of our fertility problems. We were approved for coverage on December 1 and found out we were pregnant a little over two weeks later. If we knew that we were pregnant before the first of the month, then the pregnancy would not have been covered. Dr. Ziernicki wrote a note for us confirming that we could not have known prior to the first of the month.

Upon Dr. Ziernicki's recommendation, I started taking progesterone right away. Progesterone is a hormone that supports pregnancy, specifically in the first trimester. Low levels of progesterone can cause early miscarriages.

We went in to see Dr. Ziernicki as soon as we could—four days before Christmas. They could not see a heartbeat yet in the ultrasound but saw the fetal pole and told me to come back in a couple of weeks. Dr. Ziernicki ordered bloodwork to measure my hormone levels. On New Year's Eve, I returned and had another ultrasound, which showed that the baby had grown. Based on its size, it was measuring a few days off from my date, but they weren't worried about that at the time. My progesterone level was high, but that was because of the hormone pill. My hCG levels were off, however. Although they were increasing, they were not doubling as they should in the early weeks of pregnancy.

Dr. Ziernicki was compassionate but pessimistic. She said, "I hope this isn't what I think it may be indicating. We'll have to wait and see …" I was devastated. However, a few hours later, the nurse practitioner called, not knowing I had already spoken to Dr. Ziernicki. She was much more hopeful and said, "At least your levels are going up and all you can do is try not to worry." That was exactly what I needed to hear. I tried to be patient and to trust God. After all, He healed my heart after the miscarriages, and I was filled with hope that this pregnancy would be different. I longed to have a baby that I could meet and hold.

In January, we had another ultrasound—at the eight-week mark. I was full of doubt and discouragement. However, this time there was a heartbeat! We were so happy to see it, yet I still feared that we were going to lose this baby too. Dr. Ziernicki suggested that we wait until the twelve-week ultrasound appointment to see how the baby was developing.

THE TWELVE-WEEK APPOINTMENT

The twelve-week appointment had finally come. Brian and I went to see Dr. Ziernicki on February 20, 2014—the day before my thirty-third birthday and around the one-year anniversary of our first miscarriage with Daniel. I got a call from the doctor's office earlier that day to notify me that Dr. Ziernicki had to perform an emergency C-section. They wanted to know if I would like to reschedule or keep my appointment but see a different doctor. I definitely wanted to go that day. I sat in the waiting room, praying for good news.

We started off—of course—with an ultrasound. I was so nervous having been through so many bad ones by now. The tech took a look, and we saw the heartbeat! We made it to the twelve-week mark with a heartbeat! She said the heart rate was normal and things were looking good. She said that the fetus was measuring a couple days smaller than expected based on my dates, but that was not a problem.

We returned to the waiting room before seeing the doctor. Even though the tech said the ultrasound looked okay, I was still worried. *What about my hormone levels? Why were they off?* Brian turned to me and reassured, "See, everything is going to be fine." Those words did not help at all. I had a nagging feeling that something was wrong. After going through two miscarriages in a row, I felt so fragile. I wanted the doctor to unequivocally tell me everything was fine.

We were called back to the exam room and saw a young doctor, Dr. Henderson. She came in right away with the ultrasound printout in her hand. Her smiled was forced, and her skin was flushed. Looking incredibly nervous, she said she needed to talk to us about the results because she saw some things that were concerning. Her hands trembled as she pointed to the ultrasound image. She explained that there was a large nuchal fold, or a fluid sac, in the back of the baby's neck, which could be a sign of a genetic problem. She also said the feet appeared to be rounded, called "rocker bottom" feet, which was another sign of a problem. And finally, she said the size of the fetus was actually a week off, which was significant for that early in the pregnancy.

I could not contain my tears as she gave details about each area of concern. She said, "Having one of these results is not always indicative of a problem, but because there are multiple signs, I recommend that you see a specialist and have a high-definition ultrasound done." She handed me a card for Denver Reproductive Specialists, a maternal-fetal medicine clinic for high-risk pregnancies.

Stunned, we managed to finish our appointment. All I wanted to do was escape and weep in private. Being part of a medical co-op, we pay as we go and get a discount at our doctor's office if we pay the same day. *Why did we care to get the dumb discount?* In hindsight, it was foolish to go through the hassle after getting such devastating news. I sat in a chair in the lobby and unsuccessfully tried to hold back tears while Brian paid. The moment we walked out the door of the office and into the hallway, I fell apart. We sobbed and he held me. I cried all the way home. I also called the specialty clinic because it was almost closing time. They had an appointment either the next morning, my birthday, or on the following Monday. I did not want to wait the weekend with the potential bad news looming out there, so I made the appointment for Friday, February 21.

DENVER REPRODUCTIVE SPECIALISTS

Brian did not have a lot of flexibility with his job at the time and could not make a morning appointment. He understood that I did not want to wait, so I brought my mom for support. I went to work for a couple of hours that morning—*again, why didn't I just take the day off?* But I liked my job and wanted to do something normal to pass the time.

Mom met me at Denver Reproductive Specialists (DRS), and we sat in the waiting room. DRS is a large maternal-fetal medicine clinic in the Denver area with several locations. They see women with high-risk pregnancies—high risk for the baby or for the mother. There were two other women in the waiting room. Women are weird—we strike up totally intimate, inappropriate conversations with each other even though we are strangers. I know—it's called "The Sisterhood," but that day it was horrible to be near it. The two other women were both pregnant with twins and excitedly comparing stories and belly sizes. I felt crushed listening to their joyful chatter while I waited for news to either confirm or contradict what we were told the day before.

Mom and I were called back for the ultrasound. The tech took a look first and then called the doctor in. Her name was Dr. Bedi. She was beautiful and exotic-looking and wore large diamond jewelry. I hated her. She explained that what she saw was very concerning. During early development, when the spinal cord is formed, a sac of fluid can develop at the base of the neck. Normally it is small and, in some cases, even when it is larger, it can just go away. But Dr. Bedi was also concerned about the positioning of our baby's hands and feet as well as its small size. Somehow, she could also tell that the heart did not look right, and as early as it was, she was concerned about the formation of its lungs.

Dr. Bedi said that this combination of problems can be indicative of a serious genetic problem—the most common being trisomy 13, trisomy 18, or trisomy 21 (Down syndrome). She said that trisomy 21 was the least serious, and the other potential ones were "non-life compatible." That was the first of many times when I heard that awful phrase. Non-life compatible. What a horrible, sterile term. *Non-life compatible. Meaning … your baby isn't going to survive …*

She asked, "What do you want to do about the pregnancy?" I suspected she was trying to feel out if we would want to terminate it but could not directly ask. It was very irritating. Hotly, I said, "As long as the baby has a heartbeat, we would never consider ending it."

I was almost thirteen weeks along, so Dr. Bedi recommended either doing a CSV or amniocentesis to get more information about what was going on. As result of everything we had been through, I felt like I practically had my own fetal-maternal medical degree. CVS, short for chorionic villus sampling, is a procedure, typically done in the first trimester, in which the doctor takes a sample of the placenta to test its genetic makeup. The placenta actually carries the genetic material of the future baby because it is made from the sperm and egg coming together.

Now you may be wondering, how does the doctor get some of a woman's placenta? He or she inserts a catheter into the vagina, through the cervix and into the uterus! That's right—it's incredible what medical procedures can do and incredibly unpleasant at the same time. Of course, there are risks involved with entering the womb—the chance of miscarriage is about one out of one hundred. And sometimes the results get contaminated with the mother's genetic material, which can produce a false result.

My other option was to have an amniocentesis since I was close to the second trimester. But I didn't want to wait, and there was a small risk of miscarriage with that procedure as well. I laughed a bit to myself with how seriously Dr. Bedi explained the risk of miscarriage—after she had practically just asked us if we would consider an abortion. *So now she wanted me to worry about a miscarriage instead?!* I felt like she was implying that an abortion would be okay, but a miscarriage would be a loss. That was the least of my worries at that point. We potentially had a "non-life compatible baby," for heaven's sake!

While trying to take in what Dr. Bedi was explaining to me, I cried—hard. Mom hugged me, and I was glad she was there.

We went back to the waiting room to pay and schedule the CVS. Mom hugged me again, and I cried some more. I tried to hold it together, but the feelings were too strong. I cried in the waiting room. I wept in the hallway. I sobbed in the parking lot. Mom offered to stay with me, but I wanted to get in my car and call Brian to tell him about the appointment. He answered my call, and I just bawled, unable to get the words out to explain what we were just told. He cried, too, after deciphering what I was trying to tell him.

And then it was still my birthday. Celebrating was the last thing I wanted to do. Nevertheless, I went through the motions. I pretended to enjoy dinner out and choked down some cake as I remembered our last miscarriage and wondered what would happen with our current pregnancy. It was a horrible birthday.

MAKING SENSE OF THE NEWS

That weekend, we cried and tried to recover from the news. On Monday, I called Dr. Ziernicki to request a prescription for Zofran, an anti-nausea medication. Despite what we just learned, I still had morning sickness, and a little life was growing inside of me. With Constance, I had terrible morning sickness and toughed it out the entire time. As soon as we got the news that something was seriously wrong, I thought—*nuts to that, I am not going to make this pregnancy any harder than it has to be.* Competing for the Most Nauseated Mom Award is only fun when you have the hope of a healthy baby, and morning sickness is your only problem. While I was pregnant with Constance, I craved anything dairy, but especially cottage cheese. I ate my way through it by the pound. For this pregnancy, I craved Skittles, which Brian benefitted from too. With the bad news, I did not hold myself back!

We pondered the information that we received at the two appointments: Our baby was going to have serious defects because of its genetic condition. The possibilities had been laid out before us by Dr. Bedi:

1. We could choose to terminate the pregnancy OR
2. We might end up miscarrying naturally OR
3. We could have a stillborn baby OR
4. We could end up raising a severely disabled child

Of all those awful options, having a miscarriage sounded like a blessing, even though I knew they were horrible. Terminating the pregnancy just wasn't an option we would consider, and I didn't want to give birth to a stillborn baby. As I wrestled with our situation over the following weeks and months, I prayed so hard for a miscarriage. *God, please give me the easy way out of this ...*

Amidst the bad news, there was some hope. Our baby had a strong heartbeat, which I was grateful for. As much as I prayed for a miscarriage, I also deeply longed to have a baby that I could hold, no matter the outcome. I didn't get to meet Daniel or Sarah. That longing gave me a tremendous amount of strength to carry on with the pregnancy.

WAITING ON A DIAGNOSIS

The chorionic villus sampling procedure was scheduled for the following Thursday, February 27. We planned it so Brian could come this time. I went to work that morning as if nothing was unusual for the day. *Why didn't I take the day off? Get a pedicure and a latte?* Hindsight.

Dr. Bedi recommended that another doctor in the clinic should do the procedure because he had more experience. I had never been to a male gynecologist, and I tried to remember he looks at hoo-hoos all day, and this is normal for him. But it was still a little weird. We went into the ultrasound room for the procedure. The doctor used the ultrasound screen to guide him as the ultrasound tech, Brian, and I watched. I stopped watching and just stared at the ceiling as the catheter entered my uterus. Brian continued to watch the screen. It did not feel good at all, but it was a success from a medical standpoint.

They told us that the results would come back in two parts. We would get "the rapid results" back within a few days for the major genetic disorders and then a couple of weeks later, we would get the full results. The next few days were a blur of trying to make sense of what we had been told so far. It was incomprehensible to me. I remember my mind racing, yet landing on nothing, like when you are trying to find a radio station while driving through the desert.

We told our pastor and the elders at church, as well as friends and family, and they started praying for us immediately. We felt incredibly blessed to know so many people who we could reach out to and know that they would fervently pray on their knees for strength, healing, health, and God's wisdom and mercy for us.

I was particularly touched by my friend Ginger's reaction. The weekend after we got the initial bad news, we hosted a ten-year reunion party for our former singles group. We were now all paired off, married, and had a slew of ankle-biters. It was wonderful chaos to have about fifteen products of our marriages, all under age five, crawling around. I told some of the women there what was going on. Ginger, a beautiful woman on the inside and out, was especially moved by our news and started crying as I told her what we were expecting to go through in the coming months. I was blessed by her unwavering support, prayer, encouragement, and listening ear throughout the rest of our pregnancy. I was amazed at her compassion and empathy, especially because she had not gone through an experience like this herself.

She was one of many special people who walked beside me, carrying me at times. I am so grateful for how God puts people like her in our lives to be His hands and feet. That is one of His great mercies during times of hardship.

MARCH 2014

We had a big family trip planned at the beginning of March to celebrate Brian's grandmother's ninetieth birthday in Virginia. The birthday celebration also fell on our wedding anniversary, March 8. The day before we left for the trip, while doing chalk with Constance on the driveway, I got a call from a medical assistant at DRS. I could immediately tell by the tone of her voice and the fact that the doctor was not calling that she thought she was delivering good news. She said that the results did not show any genetic abnormality for the most common genetic disorders. I did not feel relieved by this news at all. Dr. Bedi painted such a bleak picture that obviously something serious was wrong. The medical assistant said the full results would come back in another week, which would be while we were on our trip. I knew I would keep my phone at my side as much as I could, waiting for the call.

The trip was pretty normal, but traveling made my morning sickness even worse. It was hard to process the news while being with Brian's relatives, some of whom I didn't know that well. The girlfriend of one of Brian's cousins was pregnant with a healthy baby that was about as far along as I was, which was a hard comparison. But Brian's brother, Greg, and his wife, Amanda, whom we are really close to, were also there, and they were a great support to us.

We didn't find out the full results until we returned home. This time, I got a call from Dr. Bedi herself. She said some abnormalities came back, indicating a problem with chromosome 18. However, she said the results were mixed, and she was not sure how to interpret it. She recommended that we go see a genetic counselor to analyze the results.

GENETIC TESTING RESULTS

We met with the genetic counselor, Kathy, at the DRS office near downtown Denver in mid-March. Kathy showed us the karyotype from the CVS. I needed a quick refresher from high school biology on chromosomes. Humans have twenty-three pairs of chromosomes, including the XX chromosome if you are a female and XY chromosome if you are a male. Each chromosome looks like an X, with two short arms and two long arms (although it makes more sense to me to think of them as legs). They float around in your cells and then when the testers get a sample, they organize them on a chart to see what is there. Kathy explained that our results showed a mix of chromosomes called mosaicism (yeah—like an art project). Some of the cells obtained showed monosomy 18, meaning there was only one chromosome 18. Some cells were normal with two chromosomes, and some showed trisomy 18, meaning there was an extra chromosome 18. The results were clouded by the fact that the trisomy chromosomes and monosomy chromosome weren't complete. The short arm of the eighteenth chromosome was missing, or there was an extra long arm for the third chromosome copy.

Kathy said that she had never seen cells with this specific result in her ten years of testing and therefore did not totally know how to interpret it in respect to our baby's development. She did say, though, that trisomy 18 is not an inherited disorder. It is a fluke of cell division. She said that the level of disability that our child would have depends on when and where the fluke occurred. Trisomy cells in the brain, heart, and other organs would lead to a worse outcome than in the arms, for example. She also said that the monosomy cells were not as deadly as the trisomy cells. And finally, the cells with a normal set of chromosomes could temper the effect of the cells that were missing or had an extra copy of the parts of the chromosomes.

The results were interesting, yet overwhelming. I craved a definitive answer for what was going to happen, but we didn't get one.

We left the meeting without the concrete conclusion we were looking for. What we did get, however, was a bunch of handouts about trisomy 18 and various support groups. I put them in a nice little binder that I had created and then put the binder away in my closet, with no plans to read it. It was clear that we were going to have A LOT of doctor appointments, and I tried to stay organized.

DWELLING IN THE RICHNESS OF GOD'S MERCY

For most of this pregnancy, we just wanted a clear answer for what was going to happen. We wanted to know what to expect. As the weeks moved forward, we never got that clarity. The only thing we were consistently told by the medical providers was that it was going to be bad—one way or another—and that our precious baby was very sick.

The fact that the results were not clear gave us an opportunity to pray for God's mercy, goodness and for His plan. We shared the results that were known so far with family and friends. The elders of our church, with their wives, came over several times over the next few months to pray for us. I recalled the Bible study many years ago when I heard about the woman who carried a terminal pregnancy, and remembered how, at the time, I thought that was one of the most horrible experiences one could go through. As that became a possibility for us, I felt oddly prepared for it—I guess as much as one can be. I had just gone through two pregnancy losses in a row, and I figured that since I was able to get through those, I was going to get through this. God would continue to be with me. I also drew strength to get through it because I desperately wanted to have a baby that I could meet and hold, no matter the outcome.

I truly felt that God gave me supernatural emotional strength to handle this pregnancy. I remember going for a run at about four months along in the pregnancy (*impressive, I know*) and crying out to God as I processed what we were going through. At the same time, I praised Him for the situation because I felt His presence more strongly than I had ever felt it before. It was as if His Spirit poured out from heaven and covered me. Romans 8:38–39 says:

> "For I am convinced that neither death nor life, neither angels nor demons, neither the present nor the future, nor any powers, neither height nor depth, nor anything else in all creation, will be able to separate us from the love of God that is in Christ Jesus our Lord."

I felt that it was worth it to go through such a horrible earthly experience because God was merciful enough to reveal His surpassingly wonderful, powerful presence, which made the awful things we were experiencing pale in comparison. That knowledge, combined with our faith in Jesus Christ and the hope of meeting our child, gave me the strength to carry on with the pregnancy, despite all the doom and gloom that the doctors bestowed upon us at each appointment.

SIXTEEN WEEKS

The week after we met with the genetic counselor, we had our sixteen-week appointment with Dr. Bedi at DRS, followed by our regular sixteen-week appointment with Dr. Ziernicki. That made for six appointments in about a four-week span. That day, Brian met me at home, and we drove over to the DRS office together. The medical assistant called us back to the room for a vaginal ultrasound with Dr. Bedi—they did not even start with the technician this time. She explained that things were continuing to develop as expected.

Trying to hold on to a bit of hope, I asked if the baby's limbs could start to grow the way they should or if the heart and brain would catch up developmentally, instead of continuing to get worse. Dr. Bedi sadly shook her head.

We sat in the dimly lit ultrasound room, and she went over the grim details of all the ways the heart was not developing correctly. As I tried to think of questions to ask and absorb the technical information, I looked over at Brian, who was very quiet. Turns out he was more than just quiet—HE WAS ASLEEP! We were learning devastating information about our baby while I had a probe up my hoo-hoo, and he was asleep in the chair! To be a little fair, he had gotten up around 3:00 a.m. for work (his normal schedule—*yuck*), the room was warm and dark, and his chair was cushioned, *but still— come on!* A swift whack on the shoulder woke him up to two women giving him dirty looks. I was so mad at him after our appointment that I very seriously considered leaving him at the curb and letting him figure out how to get home. It took a few days before we made up.

That following Monday, we had our appointment with Dr. Ziernicki. It was such a comfort to see her, but the appointment also seemed redundant. I was going to talk to Dr. Ziernicki about just switching to DRS to simplify, but she beat me to it. She reviewed our ultrasound and gave me the chance to talk about it and ask her any additional questions. She gave me a hug and did not charge us for the visit.

It was hard to say goodbye to Dr. Ziernicki. She was so kind and compassionate, but she agreed that I needed a specialist. It felt like we were acknowledging the seriousness of our situation and admitting that our need was greater than what a regular OB-GYN handles. This was our third pregnancy with Dr. Ziernicki, and I was disappointed that she was not going to deliver a baby for us yet again.

NAMING MICHAEL JAIR

After all these appointments and sharing updates with friends and family, we felt that we needed a name for our baby so that we could reference him by name. We had found out it was a boy with the CVS results. The staff at DRS asked us if we wanted to wait to find out the gender, but that game is only fun with a healthy pregnancy, not when the baby's life is on the line. Brian's dad is named Michael, and I liked traditional boy names. Brian really liked the name Jair, who was a judge in the

Old Testament. I was willing to concede on the condition that it was a middle name!

Naming our babies in utero made it much more personal and easier to bond with them. It also made our prayers feel so much more powerful and intimate—a reminder that God knits us in the womb and knows us already. It acknowledges that they really are little people in there, with souls, created by God.

WRESTLING WITH THE PROGNOSIS

As the shock of the past four weeks of testing and results sunk in, life settled down into the normal rhythm of pregnancy—almost. As I moved into the middle of the second trimester, I started feeling better physically and also started to feel Michael move. And that is when I started experiencing the duality of our pregnancy. From this point on, life was normal and pretty good between appointments—until we inevitably had our next doctor's appointment and the cruel reality of whatever horrible outcome was waiting for us seemed to rise up and slap us in the face.

A pattern emerged: We would attend an appointment, hear what terrible things were going on in utero and the myriad of things that were not developing right, and still not receive a conclusive answer from the doctor about what to expect. Each time, it took a few days to emotionally recover as we drifted back into normal life.

We received so much information from those first six appointments, yet also felt like we received nothing definitive about Michael's life. Was the prognosis more like monosomy

18, and he would live but be disabled? Or was his prognosis more like trisomy 18, and those fateful words, "non-life compatible," that I first heard a month ago would apply to our situation? Would we bring him home from the hospital? Would he make it to his first birthday? Would our lives be drastically changed by raising a child with special needs? And if so, how severe? Would he be able to play Special Olympics or would that be beyond his capabilities? Would we need to plan a funeral for him? Was Michael going to live or die? It was hard to even accept that we needed to explore these questions. Just thinking about them was emotionally exhausting.

As challenging as these questions were, I could not actually picture him dying. I could not picture our life after birth at all. When I thought about it, my mind just went blank. All I could visualize was a sea of white. At the same time, I found my mind drifting toward details of a funeral. It felt very surreal.

Yet, as I said, I was feeling pretty good physically, which was a blessing so that I could have the strength to cope mentally. While I had no idea what was going to happen after birth, I was pretty sure breastfeeding was not an option. I figured that most likely, he would be too ill to latch or in the NICU for too long. I gained almost forty pounds with Constance, and even with burning extra calories from breastfeeding, it still took two years to get back to pre-pregnancy weight. This time, I was much more conscious of trying not to gain more weight than what was recommended.

I also decided that I was going to enjoy this pregnancy as much as possible, because this may be the best part of Michael's life that we would get to experience. I got rid of any maternity clothes that I didn't like (*you know what I am talking about—all pregnant women have them*) and decided I would be the cutest preggo lady anyone had ever seen. After all, that is one of the few fun things about being pregnant.

Somewhere along the way, we started going out to dinner after doctor appointments. Each appointment was so draining that it was nice not to have to worry about cooking dinner for our family. And as wonderful and helpful as Brian is, cooking is not his strong suit (although he would do it if I asked because he is the best husband ever).

Also in this time period, I started enjoying a glass of wine after appointments. *Yes, I know drinking is not advised.* I did not do it in the first trimester, but having a baby that was missing part of his brain gives you a bit of a reality check on all the restrictions that the doctors give you regarding the health of your baby.

TWENTY WEEKS

We had our twenty-week appointment at DRS with Dr. Bedi, and then we met with a nurse practitioner afterward. Dr. Bedi did the ultrasound, and I was honestly hoping that something had changed for the better. All Dr. Bedi kept saying over and over, rather emphatically, was, "This is bad." I am always amazed at how much information doctors glean from an ultrasound. To me, it is just a fuzzy, black-and-white screen. I can see the baby's outline, but that's about it.

Dr. Bedi launched into all the problems she was seeing. First, she talked about Michael's hands and feet. All four limbs were growing at severely contorted angles. I asked Dr. Bedi, "Could they be fixed surgically?" Dr. Bedi responded, "There are more concerning things to talk about," and she moved on to his heart.

Dr. Bedi explained that the left side of his heart was much bigger than the right. The right side pumps blood throughout the body, but in Michael's case, his heart would most likely be too small to do so. She also explained that both of the major arteries were coming from the left side, rather than one from the left and one from the right. Also, there were holes between the ventricles, so unoxygenated blood would enter the wrong chamber. She said heart surgery after birth could be an option, but most likely it would require multiple surgeries to correct it. She said that this ultrasound also confirmed what she suspected from our last one—that the frontal lobe of Michael's brain appeared to be missing.

"What are the implications of that?" I asked, knowing this was very serious.

She said, "If your baby were to survive, he would be very disabled."

"How disabled? Like walking and talking or confined to a wheelchair?"

She looked me in the eye and said straightforwardly, "He would not be able to interact with us at all. He would be in a permanent vegetative state."

It felt like the rug was pulled out from under us. My heart dropped into my gut. I barely heard her as she continued to say, "It looks like there are problems with his lungs, but those develop later, so we will just have to wait and see how those progress." *Great, more bad news to look forward to.*

Even with Michael's dismal prognoses, we once again told Dr. Bedi that we were going to continue with the pregnancy. She said that as it got closer to the birth, we would need to decide how much intervention we would want. She said one option would be for "comfort measures only."

Those words hit me hard. I have worked with older adults my entire career, and I know what that means. *Terminal condition. Hospice. Comfort measures only.* The goal is not to cure, but to treat symptoms and let nature take its course. We squarely fell into being eligible for perinatal hospice, a combination of words that I didn't even know existed. In my mind, I freaked out. *Hospice?! No, no, no! Hospice is for my elderly clients. For the families that I support as a professional. There is no way that hospice applies to us. How could this be our reality?*

The future for baby Michael seemed so uncertain to me. I held on to the fact that since he did not have a classic diagnosis of trisomy 18, we did not know what was going to happen after he was born. I didn't think that Michael was going to die. And when I did briefly consider it, I felt I had no idea when that would happen. How could my body be a vessel for a new life that, at the same time, might be drawing to an end? I was literally a walking contradiction. In my mind, death was not possible.

After we met with Dr. Bedi, we met one of the two nurse practitioners at DRS. She was nice and gave us a brochure for an organization called String of Pearls. String of Pearls supports women carrying a pregnancy with a terminal diagnosis. I appreciated the gesture and took the pamphlet, but I did not feel that it applied to us. After all, we did not know what was going to happen after birth. When Brian and I got married, he told me he pictured life after the wedding like the rapture—life on earth as he knew it simply ended. I pictured giving birth much like that—I could not envision a single thing—just empty white space.

The appointment ended and we left. As we walked into the parking lot, we looked at each other and burst into laughter. The appointment was so heavy, so bleak and dark, that it was all we could do to blow off some emotion. We laughed at how circuitously she tried to imply we should end the pregnancy. We laughed at how many times Dr. Bedi said the word bad—such an elementary, non-medical descriptor from such an educated woman. *Yeah, lady, we get it. But we still aren't going to end the pregnancy, as dumbfounding as that may be to you.* We laughed because we were going to keep this pregnancy, no matter what!

ABORTION

From the twelve-week appointment and on, the doctors always suggested in varying degrees of overtness that terminating the pregnancy was an option. Each appointment now culminated with the doctor explaining all the things that were not developing right and ended with the big question—are you really going to continue this pregnancy? I found it noteworthy that the doctors never used the million-dollar word—that must be an ethical no-no. They tried to explain how horrible it would be to raise a disabled child or have a child die. Maybe they were trying to make sure we had the full picture to make an informed decision, but it did not feel like that. True—it's not what I signed up for, but do you really want me to stop the heartbeat that is inside of me? Do you think that you know what is better for me than what God knows? The entire time, we made it clear that we would not end it. We never considered it.

I felt angry that they presented abortion as the better choice. How shortsighted of the doctors to think that ending a pregnancy would be the "easier" option. I'll admit, in some ways it sounded good. It was tempting to believe that ending it would have stopped the pain. But that's a lie.

While it was incredibly frustrating to have to take a stand each time, it was also easy. Our belief in the sanctity of life guided our decision and the plan of care, rather than the medical prognosis. I was grateful that we could fall back on our beliefs, which are grounded in God's truth, to guide us in this hard time, rather than trying to figure out what was right in the midst of an emotional crisis.

OUTWARD SIGNS OF PREGNANCY

Around this time, Constance noticed my belly growing. She was almost three and absolutely adorable. One day, I was getting something out of the fridge, and she saw my profile. Her brown eyes grew large. "Mommy, why is your stomach so big?!" We explained to her that a baby was growing in my tummy, but he was sick. That was enough of an explanation for her.

While it was easy to give Constance a satisfying answer about our pregnancy, adults were a lot harder to deal with. As the weeks moved forward and I began to show more and more, the pregnancy started getting harder emotionally. At first, we could keep our terrible situation private and choose when and with whom to share. But as my stomach grew, it seemed to be acceptable for people to comment on my pregnancy. The problem was that most people assumed things were good—why wouldn't you in modern America?

People would ask, "Are you having a boy or a girl?" That question was easy enough, and I would tell them it's a boy. The problem was that the questions did not stop there. "Oh, boys are trouble. He is going to be running around all over the place." *No, actually he won't, because his legs are deformed.* "Your kids are going to fight, and it will drive you crazy!" *No, they won't. Our baby will be non-verbal.* Or people would ask, "Are you excited?" *Well, we would be, except we don't know if we are going to leave the hospital with our baby.*

There were two options for responding to people's comments. One was to go along with it, which really just hurt on the inside, because I was entering into a false storyline of joy and happiness that did not match our reality. The other option was to tell the truth, "The doctors are concerned that there are some serious problems, and we are not sure if he is going to live." That just left people in shock and then they felt bad. Or it opened people up to asking a lot of questions that I definitely did not want to answer.

The WORST response from others was when people tried to be encouraging by telling me some pregnancy story based on medical knowledge from thirty years ago when their cousin's daughter's friend's baby wasn't supposed to have a kidney and turns out the doctors were wrong. *Well, sorry— they can tell a lot more nowadays, and our baby's problems are a lot worse than that.*

Probably the dumbest comment I got was from a sweet, well-meaning girl in my office who was just out of college. She gently asked if I was taking my prenatal vitamins, as if to suggest that would truly make a difference. That question was actually so stupid that it didn't even bother me.

String of Pearls, the perinatal hospice organization that I contacted, later suggested that I just say, "There are some health concerns but I don't really want to talk about it." That was such a good, neutral response. I was not very good at remembering that and delivering the line at the right time, however.

Brian was fortunate. He could go to work and avoid our situation for eight hours a day. The people he encountered did not even know his wife was pregnant. But for me, there was no hiding it. To make it worse, I was in sales and marketing (which I really liked) but that meant I encountered dozens of people a day, and a different group of people day in and day out as I covered all one hundred of my accounts.

I grouped people into three categories—strangers, who unknowingly made insensitive comments that I could brush off because I would never see them again; good friends, to whom I wanted to tell the full story and have their support; and then people in the middle—those whom I would see again so I could not just act as if everything was normal, but to whom I didn't really want to reveal the whole situation. The last group was the hardest to negotiate. It took a lot of emotional energy to deal with them, whether it was sharing all, part, or none of our story.

Besides navigating the interactions with others, I wanted to enjoy the pregnancy as much as possible. A part of me realized this may be the only time I would ever have with my son. I loved feeling Michael move, just like any mother does. He seemed so healthy in my belly—*could what the doctors were saying actually be true?*

Constance was great at keeping some normalcy in the pregnancy. We started calling her a big sister. She would bring Michael toys to play with while he was in my belly and talk to him. She liked feeling him kick too. She would put her hand on my stomach and pretend that his kicks knocked her over. She would fall down and laugh, and we would do it over and over again. I loved it. As the pregnancy progressed, we reminded Constance that not all of Michael's body parts were growing the way they should, and he was not healthy. She was okay with that.

SUFFERING AND SUPPORT

At one point, Mom asked me if I was suffering. I told her no. I thought of suffering as something that happened to people who were tortured—victims of war, famine, or abuse—but not me. Looking back, I'd now say that I was suffering. I could have benefited from counseling to talk to someone about all the difficult things that we were encountering, from the awkward social interactions to approaching birth and an outcome that was unknown. But at the same time, I know why I did not consider it. It would have been too traumatic to try to process what was going on. I had to just get through it. If I stopped to process it, I don't think I could have continued. Looking back, I could have used some sort of guidance, even if it was someone just telling me to take it easy.

While I did not rely on counseling, our marriage was a tremendous source of strength for me. I cannot imagine going through this without a strong partner. Every night before bed, Brian and I would take time to "talk about our feelings," which really meant me talking about my feelings and him listening to me. But to be fair, we both would share what we were thinking as the pregnancy went on. We continued doing this after Michael was born and still do it now. On really bad days, though, we would skip talking. It was too hard. Instead, we would purposely escape reality by watching a favorite TV show on Netflix before going to bed, and that escape was helpful too.

We had been urged to contact String of Pearls at our twenty-week appointment after we made it clear for the umpteenth time that we were going to continue the pregnancy. While I felt confident that we didn't want to end the pregnancy, I did not want to contact them. Facing what might happen to us was too hard. I could not bring myself to acknowledge that Michael might die.

One day, however, I went on the String of Pearls website and read every word on it. The organization was named after the founder's daughter, Pearl, who had a terminal diagnosis in utero and was not expected to live after birth. Pearl's mother, Laura Huene, BSN, RN, chose to carry Pearl to term and subsequently started String of Pearls to support parents who found themselves in the same situation. The website said that the goal of String of Pearls is to help parents navigate "the fine line between grief and hope in a pregnancy." It perfectly described how I felt. It was natural and necessary for me to be hopeful. If I did not have hope, I could not have carried on. Proudly (or because of pure denial), I did not want to work with String of Pearls because I truly thought there was a good chance that Michael would live. I did not want to utilize their services if it did not apply to me. But at the same time, we could not ignore the reality of what we were going through or being told about the future. I wept as I began to consider the wonderful services that they offered.

Around twenty-two weeks, I got the courage to call String of Pearls and spoke to Laura, the founder and an angel in human form. She simply listened to my story. She was very understanding and supportive. She only offered advice when I asked and spoke with me from my reality of believing that he would live. After we spoke, she sent me a large package, which I did not have the nerve to open. I put it, unopened, in the room that was to be Michael's nursery.

TWENTY-FOUR WEEKS

After the twenty-week appointment, DRS wanted me to start coming in every two weeks to be checked by the nurse practitioner. That was okay with me. I liked getting information, even if it was "bad." But Brian didn't like it. He didn't like hearing the same news over and over again. He was strongly against having a twenty-four-week ultrasound appointment because any new information was not going to impact our course of action. He was right, but I craved learning more about our baby. The nurse practitioner gave me a quick peek with their basic ultrasound machine to check my fluid at the bi-weekly appointments, so I got to see baby Michael that way. I liked it.

I heeded Brian's wish to skip the official twenty-four-week appointment. DRS said that was okay, but we would have to discuss some things soon in order to plan for the medical care that Michael might need after birth. Instead of having an ultrasound, we followed DRS's advice to start preparing for delivery.

DRS let us know that they only deliver at Presbyterian St. Luke's Hospital (PSL) in Denver. We had a great experience giving birth to Constance at Parker Adventist Hospital, and I asked if that would be a possibility. DRS explained that most area hospitals did not handle high-risk pregnancies. I found that surprising because one would think they could handle it by the way they advertise their state-of-the-art facilities, NICU, and trained staff. All the hospitals do a ton of marketing to expectant mothers because labor and delivery is such a moneymaker.

We were assigned a hospital liaison who suggested we come in for a tour of the delivery unit. Brian and I drove forty minutes from our house to the downtown hospital. The liaison met us at the St. Luke's DRS office and walked us over to the hospital itself. PSL is one of the oldest hospitals in Denver. Unlike the bright and spacious halls at the newer hospitals near us, PSL was a labyrinth of dark, narrow, twisting hallways.

Our liaison explained that since the unit was retrofitted to accommodate a growing practice as a result of the advancement of medicine, the labor and delivery unit was actually in a different tower than the NICU. She said that depending if Michael had to be whisked off for treatment after birth, Brian would go with him, and I would be alone to recover. That sounded horrible, but of course, I would not want Michael to be alone. As the tour continued, she explained about all the specialists they had—combinations of medical jargon that I never had thought of—pediatric cardiologists and neonatal pulmonologists and so forth.

Being on the labor and delivery unit made it feel like we were coming to the end of our journey very soon. It felt like we were starting to run, rather than walk, toward those two horrible doors—death or disability. I hit my emotional limit when we reached the neonatal hospice room. The rest of the rooms looked like normal labor and delivery hospital rooms. We were now standing in a special room on the floor that looked more like a cozy hotel room with a double bed, a nightstand and a lamp, and a rug. The liaison explained that this room was for parents whose baby was too sick to leave the hospital, and it gave the parents the chance to stay with their child as their son or daughter died. I lost it. I sat on the bed and wept. It was just too much to face.

In a few weeks, we would have our twenty-eight-week ultrasound appointment and, based on the information we got from that, we would need to start meeting with the various specialists to learn our treatment options and decide how aggressive with care we would want to get. Who wants to have to decide if they want CPR for their newborn?! It was heart-breaking. I didn't even know what our choices were, but I knew the information would be excruciating to think about. I did not want to decide about heart surgery for our baby—I wanted a healthy baby. I sat in the hospice room and cried for a while, then we finished the tour.

From the moment we broke the news to our family and friends, people had been holding us up in prayer. They prayed for my health, for Michael, for our marriage, for our spirits, and they also prayed for a miracle. This experience challenged my belief in miraculous healing. I was afraid to pray for it. I know that God is all-powerful and able to perform miracles, but I have never witnessed a healing firsthand. I wrestled with the falsehood that if I just believed enough, prayed enough, and trusted enough, that God would heal us. I was afraid that God's action depended on my faith, rather than on His omnipotence and mercy.

As we drove home from the hospital tour, I admitted my fear to Brian. "What if God heals Michael only enough so that he lives but is severely disabled?" I knew we would love him and care for him regardless, but it was not what I wanted. Brian told me that if God chose to heal him, He would heal him completely and not halfway. We just needed to trust. That night we went out for dinner, and I enjoyed a well-earned margarita—big belly and all.

With the tour behind us, we had a few weeks of normalcy until we had to face the next set of decisions. My dear friend

Alicia, who struggled with a special needs child of her own, asked if I wanted to do something to celebrate the pregnancy. She recognized that a normal shower, or "sprinkle," wouldn't quite be right. Deep down, I wanted to have a celebration of some kind, but I was afraid to admit that it was such a hard situation. I figured I had a few weeks to decide how we wanted to acknowledge it. I vacillated during the entire pregnancy between openly embracing what was going on or just putting my head down and trying to get through a hard situation so I didn't fall apart before the finish line. And I most definitely viewed giving birth as the finish line ...

MOM'S FALL—THE BEGINNING OF THE END

The morning of Friday, May 30, started out normal enough. Brian's dad and stepmom, Mike and Kim, had flown in from Atlanta the night before. We had a nice dinner with them on our back patio before they left to drive up to the mountains to be with friends for the weekend. Little did we know that meanwhile, my parents were having a crisis just a few miles away but did not want to call and interrupt our dinner party.

That following morning, Friday, I was waiting like usual for Mom to come over to watch Constance while I was at work. There was a knock at the door at the expected time. I opened the door and was surprised to see Dad standing there instead of Mom.

"Mom fell last night and broke both her legs. She is at the hospital now. I can take Constance and watch her there while I am with Mom." I was shocked. I had trouble comprehending the terrible news that he was telling me.

"Mom was folding laundry on the couch last night," he continued. "When she went to get up, her legs got tangled under her, and she landed directly on her kneecaps on the hardwood floor, breaking both kneecaps at the same time." It was a total freak accident. God bless my father for wanting to help me out in their time of crisis, but babysitting their grandchild was not the most important thing to focus on at that time.

As I closed the door and sent Dad away to be with Mom, I fell apart. I called into work to let them know that I would be late. *Now why in the hell did I go into work? Go easy on myself, visit Mom.* I definitely should have taken the day off. Anyone picking up on a recurring theme? I tried so hard to proceed like life was normal and not acknowledge the incredible stress facing me at every turn. I always could push myself to act as if life was fine with the hope that by ignoring my feelings, I could ignore reality. It doesn't work.

After I called the office, I called my friend Charlotte, who didn't hesitate to take Constance for the day along with her own three children. Charlotte is a dear friend from church who watched Constance in the past and has been one of my biggest sources of support.

We found out Mom needed to have double knee surgery to wire both her kneecaps together so they could heal. She would be out of commission for months. With Mom's fall, hospitalization, and subsequent double knee surgery, I lost my emotional support and my childcare at the same time. Plus, I knew then she would not be around to help when Michael was born. Although I was only twenty-seven weeks along, we knew

Michael would be born early. Babies with genetic problems are more likely to be premature, and Constance was born a month early. We just didn't realize how soon he would be coming.

Mom had her surgery on Saturday, May 31, two days after falling. Brian and I had made plans previously with my mother-in-law, Lynn, to go to the mountains to ride the Georgetown Loop Railroad, a tourist attraction. I really didn't want to be in the mountains—I wanted to be in the hospital with Mom. But we were obligated to keep our plans or face the guilt of hurting feelings, so we kept our plans. It turned out to be a fun day, but at the same time, my mind was thinking about my mom in surgery.

While this was going on with me and my family, my boss was going out of the country the following week, and I would be left in charge of the company for two weeks. Our business was home care—very tumultuous, as care is being provided around the clock in people's homes. Something was always happening to our elderly clients or with our low-wage caregivers. Things often did not go smoothly, even when the boss was in town. I did not feel confident that I could handle things while he was gone and was nervous about how much extra work it would be.

With each passing week, I felt my emotions ratchet up. As we crept closer to my due date, everything seemed harder. I had less tolerance to handle the normal challenges in a day and very little ability to handle stress.

Emotionally, I was breaking down. I felt like I lost my mom, work was overwhelming, and the question about what was going to happen to Michael was looming over me. And all the while, I was fielding more and more unknowingly irrelevant, inappropriate, and insensitive pregnancy comments as I entered the third trimester.

TWENTY-SEVEN WEEKS

I had a little bloody discharge on Sunday, June 1, but did not think much of it. I also noticed my underwear always seemed a little wet that week—I passed it off as pregnancy incontinence. We ladies go through so much to have babies!

That week, I visited mom in the hospital after her surgery and then at the skilled rehab center where she was discharged afterward. She would need five or six weeks of physical therapy to recover from her accident. She had a nice, spacious room with a comfortable recliner for me to put my feet up. Mom was so distraught that she had hurt herself so badly. It was a loss for me, too, but at least I could visit and still talk to her as we commiserated over each other's crises.

THE PLAN

Besides visiting Mom, my week was filled with work. Since I was covering for my boss, I did not go on my normal external marketing appointments. As I stayed in the office to manage issues as they came up, my thoughts drifted to the future. We were scheduled to have our twenty-eight-week appointment with DRS the following week. After that appointment, we were going to need to make some serious decisions based on the various contingencies at Michael's birth.

With each ultrasound, I always hoped for a miracle or some dramatic change. And each appointment was a sobering disappointment. A dismal reminder of what we were in for and that we were going to have to come up with a plan for how much intervention we would want for Michael. Did we want Michael intubated? Did we want him to have immediate heart surgery to save his life? Would we want oxygen or CPR? I didn't even know all the options that we would have to consider, but I knew it would be excruciating to think about. Based on the information gleaned from the twenty-eight-week ultrasound, we were going to set up appointments with a neonatal pulmonologist, a neonatal cardiologist, and who knows what other type of highly specialized physician that I didn't even know existed.

What I dreaded most was having to select a mortuary. Pregnant ladies should not have to plan their baby's funeral before they are even born. I knew his death was a realistic possibility, and I knew it would be better to plan for it ahead of time—yet mentally, I could not even go there.

SETTING UP THE NURSERY

We were not sure, of course, what would happen after birth, but I wanted to set up a nursery for Michael. I had a fierce desire to do all the normal things that one did and to enjoy the pregnancy as much as possible. We had a free evening on Thursday, June 5. We assembled Michael's crib, cleaned out the old furniture in the room, and figured out how to arrange the new furniture and rocking chair. It was fun, and the room looked nice. I felt a mix of joy and sadness looking at the empty crib—anticipating his birth with hope yet fearfully wondering if he would ever lie in it. I figured in a month or so we would know.

FRIDAY, JUNE 6

Work went pretty smoothly while my boss was out of town. That Friday, I had a normal day at work, but I did not feel too good physically. By late morning, I was starting to have very light contractions—more like Braxton Hicks, which I never had with Constance. I left work after a few hours and went home. I called DRS. They told me to lie down, drink a lot of water, and see if that made it get better. They also offered that I could come in for them to take a look. I felt better after resting and had plans to see an old college girlfriend, Melissa, and I did not want to cancel those plans. Plus, I didn't like going to DRS. *Besides,* I figured, *what could they tell me that would make a difference?* In hindsight, going to the doctor would have influenced the course of events. Melissa was about five months pregnant with her second, and we had fun chatting about our babies.

That evening, we had a special meeting with our pastor, Joe. He had a former ministry partner visiting him who had the spiritual gift of healing. Joe arranged a meeting for us to be prayed over. I was both nervous and hopeful. We met with him at our church's ministry center. Joe's friend explained how God uses healing as a testament to His power and glory and that we should pray boldly and expectantly for it. We did the best we could with the prayer, although I did not feel any different afterward. There was no tingling sensation or lightning bolt from the sky. Still, we hoped for a miracle.

A few weeks before this, our friend, James, invited us to a healing service at a charismatic church. It was a different worship style, but the people seemed genuine and not hokey. I did not go up for prayer, but enjoyed the service. Across the room, I saw a child in what looked like a wheelchair. I think it actually was a fancy stroller, but I broke down in tears when I saw it. I thought about raising a severely disabled child and how heartbreaking that would be. If Michael lived, he most certainly would be disfigured and greatly impaired physically and cognitively. I was scared to raise a disabled son, but I did not want him to die, either. Ultimately, I knew that God was with us, whether or not we had a miraculous healing.

CHAPTER FIVE

Michael's Birth

SATURDAY, JUNE 7

Since we had gone to the mountains the weekend before, and I was emotionally exhausted from the week's events, I deliberately planned a day to relax. *Finally, I did something the right way!* Saturday, June 7, was an ideal day. Brian let me sleep in, followed by a morning pedicure. I selected a deep pink, which turned out to be way too lilac for me. *Oh well, there's always next time.* That afternoon, Brian and I took Constance to a fun playground in Denver. I didn't feel too well and mostly sat while she played. We had fun as a little family of three. Then, we went out to a nice dinner to cap off a great day. All the dinner options sounded disgusting to me except for Indian food, which seemed tantalizing. It was my strongest craving so far. We went to our favorite Indian restaurant, which is owned by friends of ours. It has a great atmosphere, good food, and it's a comfortable place to be. We came home, and I went to bed early, still not feeling that well. God, who lavishes His love on us, blessed me with a day of rejuvenation in preparation for what lay ahead.

SUNDAY, JUNE 8—MICHAEL'S DAY

We went to bed Saturday night, just like normal. I woke up around 3:30 a.m. and sat up, thinking I needed to use the bathroom. Suddenly, there was a small but distinct gush of fluid. I woke up Brian immediately and told him what happened. I was not having any contractions yet. I went to the bathroom while Brian got a towel. The raindrops were starting to fall as the biggest storm in our life was about to arrive.

We called DRS and talked to a wonderful, caring nurse who was on call. We briefly told her our situation and knew we had to go to the hospital. She said, "I don't know your background but I am Christian. May I pray for you?" It was such a blessing, and I was filled with peace amidst the darkness of the night. We called Lynn, Brian's mom, and asked her to come over to finish out the night with Constance. I made a list of items I needed to bring, and Brian packed for us while I lay on our bed.

Despite the gravity of the situation, we were amused to be playing out the same movie-like scene as we did while going into labor with Constance—the not-so-little wife in labor while the frantic husband runs around and packs in the middle of the night. But unlike the brevity with Constance, there was a heaviness in the air, since Michael was sick, and I was only twenty-eight weeks along.

I started having light contractions as we left the house. We did not have a car seat for Michael, but we did not know if we would even need one. Like Constance, giving birth to Michael was wonderful, but the memory of it is also laced with so much pain. Instead of the car seat box, I threw in the unopened box from String of Pearls.

We left for the hospital around 5:00 a.m. as the sky was just starting to lighten. I knew we needed prayer, and the quickest way to get the word out was to put up a message on Facebook. I like Facebook—I think it is fun to see what friends are up to and the cute things their kids are doing. I do not like it to share sad or highly personal things. I had not even posted that I was pregnant, because I did not want all the foolish comments with hollow support from mere acquaintances. Social media can be very shallow and self-serving in those ways. But as we drove to the hospital, I wanted to quickly let as many people as possible know what was happening.

I posted at 5:32 a.m.: *Please pray. My water broke and we are going to the hospital. I am only 28 weeks.* It was short and to the point. Everyone in our church, family, and close circle of friends knew the full story about Michael and this pregnancy, but all those people who fell strictly into the "Facebook Friend" category didn't even know we were pregnant. *Oh well.*

As we drove down the highway, my contractions started getting a little more uncomfortable. Tears trickled down my cheeks as the physical pain grew. It was sinking in that this was it. It takes a lot of medical intervention to keep a healthy baby alive at twenty-eight weeks, and Michael was nowhere near healthy. I touched my belly, feeling him kick and knowing we would see him soon.

We were going to have a baby today, and he was going to die.

We pulled up to an empty ER at Presbyterian St. Luke's. We told the check-in clerk that I was in labor, and the medical tech got me into a wheelchair and up to the labor and delivery unit quicker than you could blink. Having undergone several expansions, the tech told us it was a quarter mile from the emergency room to the labor and delivery unit. He did not want anyone having a baby on his watch, and neither did I! Brian could barely keep up as we sprinted down the hall, and I held on to the armrests of my wheelchair for dear life!

We got to our room. I was starting to be in a lot of pain, but I could still feel Michael kicking. That was the last time I felt him move before the contractions took over any sensation I had. Despite the pain, the staff did not seem to be in any rush. They could not do an ultrasound or give me medicine until they had me checked into the system, so we just waited.

The plan back at home was for Lynn to take Constance to Charlotte's for the day and then Constance would sleep at Lynn's at night. By then I was crying out in pain. Brian wisely assessed how quickly things were progressing and told Lynn to come to the hospital with Constance right away. We wanted Constance to get to meet her brother, alive, and for Lynn to be there, too, since she was out of town for Constance's birth. Brian quickly called my dad and Pastor Joe, too.

Meanwhile, it felt like my sides were splitting in two. I wanted an epidural. There was no way I was toughing out this birth—the situation was hard enough in itself. The medical staff asked, in general terms, if we wanted medical treatment for Michael once he was born. We asked to have an ultrasound one more time. *Maybe God healed Michael.* We were still holding out hope for a miracle until the very end.

There was no time to be wheeled down for a full ultrasound, but they had a basic machine that they brought into the room. They moved the transducer over my abdomen, and we saw Michael for the last time inside my womb. We saw his little deformed hands and knew that God had not healed him. Brian and I looked at each other and sorrowfully said, "Comfort measures only." At that moment, it was confirmed: We were going to let Michael live and die naturally.

I was in full labor at this point, with no medication yet. Finally, the nurse got me registered and checked me. I was dilated to about four or five centimeters. The anesthesiologist came in and gave me an epidural and some wonderful Fentanyl. As the pain calmed down, my water broke completely. This time it seemed to flood the bed. It was literally a waterfall. The nurse had to entirely change me and the bedsheets. It amazes me both how disgusting labor is and that it is no big deal to the medical people. *Thank goodness!* After that, the nurse checked me again. I was dilated to nine centimeters and ready to push, but Dr. Bedi had not yet arrived. Babies do not wait for obstetricians, so they said a hospitalist was going to deliver my baby. Fortunately, Dr. Bedi arrived, and she slid into position at the very last minute.

I started pushing with the contractions. After already giving birth once, I felt like I knew how to push a baby out. I gave it my best. I sensed Michael moving down the birth canal, but for some reason, he was not coming out. *How could that be?* I was only twenty-eight weeks along, so he could not have been that big. Dr. Bedi took a closer look and realized that since Michael was small, there was more room for him to move around. He was no longer head down. He had turned, so his shoulder or arm was furthest down, and I was pushing him out sideways. Dr. Bedi told me she was going to manually rotate him. As she reached into the birth canal (*you read that right!*), she muttered under her breath, "Good thing for the epidural." After she rotated him, it only took one or two more pushes, and he was out.

The labor for Michael was fast and furious, but then once he was born and in my arms, things slowed down greatly. Brian and I started crying immediately as our precious, precious son was handed to us—our living, breathing son that we had longed to meet.

It was the culmination of not only seven hard months of pregnancy, but three years of hoping for a second child. It was the moment we were waiting for and praying for—to meet Michael alive, this side of the womb. The time that we had with him was so holy, so sacred. Surely the Holy Spirit was present in the room. I know God was in our midst; Michael was finally in my arms.

But as soon as he started living, he also started dying.

One of the neonatal doctors popped in the room, and I heard the nurse quickly say in a hushed voice, "Comfort measures."

The doctor immediately left. There was nothing medical for them to do at this point. The nurse leaned over Michael and confirmed that he had a weak heartbeat. I was so grateful that he had a pulse. He was alive. And so warm. I wrapped him up in one of the hospital blankets. He was beautiful and so tiny. His deformed little body was absolutely perfect to us.

As soon as I was cleaned up and decent, we let our family into the room: Dad, Lynn, and Constance. Lynn led Constance in by her hand. She was so calm and quiet—very atypical for a three-year-old. She was a little scared to be in the hospital and probably to see me in the bed. We introduced Constance to her brother. I handed Michael to Brian, and he helped her hold him. She was so gentle with him. She was very interested in all his body parts, spending extra time examining his feet.

The hospital chaplain came by and baptized Michael. I knew Michael was going to heaven regardless of baptism, but it was still nice to do, especially while he was still living. Coincidentally, the chaplain's name was Michael.

I passed Michael around to Dad, Lynn, Brian, and Constance. Looking back, I selfishly wish only I held him while he was alive. Yet at the same time, I wanted to share him with his family. His eyes briefly opened, and I looked into them, but I don't know if he could see me. I am not even sure if he was conscious. But he was alive.

Michael lived about twenty minutes. A lifetime lived in twenty minutes.

It wasn't obvious when he died. Those twenty minutes, along with the forty hours that we spent in the hospital, were the most intense emotions I have ever felt. We experienced the joy of meeting our child and the anguish of losing him compacted into a few minutes. All he experienced on this earth was love. I am grateful for every second of his life. I am so grateful that I met him. I am grateful that at the end of a really, really hard pregnancy, I got the incredible blessing of holding my son, alive.

Brian and Constance tenderly gave Michael a bath. He had already passed away, but washing him was such a beautiful thing to do—like the washing of Jesus' body. I just laid in bed, watching from across the room. They put a diaper on him—the tiniest diaper I had ever seen—and we wrapped him in the blue baby blanket that Lynn had knit for him.

During labor, the nurse asked me if I wanted photos from Now I Lay Me Down to Sleep—an organization in which professional photographers volunteer their time to take birth photos for babies that die. Nicole Leonard, our photographer, arrived shortly after he was born. A stranger only moments before, she played such an important role in documenting Michael's life.

I cherish the photos we have of Michael. I looked at them daily in the first year after he was born. They reminded me his life was real and not just a dream. Blending into the background, Nicole snapped away as we enjoyed our time with him. We also posed for some photos, but I didn't know if I should smile or not. *Were we happy? Sad? How did I feel? How would I want to look back on it?* I sort of gave a sad smile, as did Brian. We were happy and sad at the same time.

Our parents—Dad, Lynn, and Mark (Brian's stepdad whom we invited too)—were so loving toward Michael. Eventually, it was time for them to say goodbye. Not too long after that, Pastor Joe came. It was a stormy Sunday, and tornadoes were in the area. Joe was able to arrive by 1:00 p.m.—pretty impressive for preaching and dodging the storms. Joe prayed over Michael, and we dedicated his life to the Lord. It was nice to visit with Joe and receive his pastoral care.

After a while, Joe left and it was just the three of us. Me, Brian, and Michael. Those early hours after his birth were so tender, so cherished, and so sacred. And so short. I wished for more time. Often, when I look at the pictures that Nicole took, I literally want to pull open the picture and crawl into it. I ache to be back in those moments when I could hold Michael. That time was so raw, so vivid, so painful, yet so dear.

June 8 was the day that our son lived.

In some ways, that was the day he was real. He is still real, but now a memory. I think about him every day. I miss him so much. The feelings are so strong. *Oh Michael. Sweet Michael. Why were you so sick? I wish you could have stayed here on earth, with me.*

While we were still holding Michael, we opened the box from String of Pearls that I had received the month before. It was a lovely box—full of gifts for us and Michael. It included an ornament that you could make with his handprints. The nurses also took his hand and footprints both with ink and with plaster. Michael had a pretty good head of hair, and we cut some off and put it in an envelope. I put the box of those most precious mementos in his nursery.

I felt that since I had posted on Facebook requesting prayer on the way to the hospital, I should post an update. I knew that our friends and family were faithfully praying for us. That afternoon, I posted: *Oh FB, what a weird, efficient way to communicate. Sweet baby Michael Jair arrived at 9:44 a.m. 1 lb 11 oz. 13 inches. He went to be with the Lord shortly after. Thank you for your prayers. He was beautiful.*

The nurses at PSL were next to angels. I had two nurses assigned to me—a younger one and an older, more seasoned one—Julie Rael. Julie spent a lot of time with me. She was wonderful. She just sat on my bed with me and let me cry over Michael's body. It was the exact perfect thing to do. Just to sit, listen, and be with me as I wept and held him. Becky Barkey, a volunteer with String of Pearls, was also a nurse practitioner at PSL and came by to comfort us.

After a few hours with Michael, it seemed like time to say goodbye. How long could I hold my dead baby? I was worried about what would start to happen to his little body since he was dead. Julie told me that Michael would be kept on the unit the entire time that I was there, and we could see him any time we wanted to. I didn't think we would. He was dead, after all, and it was time to say goodbye. We cried some more, hugged Michael, and said what we thought were our final goodbyes.

That evening, things calmed down. I was exhausted from giving birth. I had lost a lot of blood in the delivery—enough to get a blood transfusion, but they recommended just letting my body recover naturally and produce more blood on its own. I wanted to see our friends James and Jane Hutcheson. Jane is one of the most significant people I have relied on through all our losses. I was friends with James from our high school youth group, and his wife, Jane, has become one of my best friends. She has had three miscarriages—two being in the second term. They came and brought me a milkshake. It was nice for the four of us to sit and talk about everything that had happened.

After they left, it was time to go to bed. I wanted to see Michael again! *How was he doing? Was he going to be okay for the night?* Just a few hours before, I thought I was going to say goodbye to him for good, but already I wanted to see and hold him again. I was his mother, and that is what mothers do—whether the child is dead or alive is irrelevant.

We had the evening nurse bring Michael back in. His body was cold, but he was wrapped in a warm blanket. I asked the nurse where he would be for the night. She said they kept him in a refrigerated area on the floor. I found that reassuring. We couldn't keep him in our room, so I was glad he was as close as he could practically be. We held him, said goodnight, and of course, cried some more.

Becky, the String of Pearls nurse practitioner, had mentioned that I may want to take some Ambien for the next few days and also start on an antidepressant. I did not think I would need either. I felt exhausted but not depressed. However, the moment I closed my weary, puffy eyes to go to sleep, I realized I was not going to be able to sleep at all. I asked the nurse for that blessed Ambien. Even with it, I remember having an unrestful night. Brian slept by my side on a pullout bed. I remember waking up in the middle of the night and weeping before I was even fully conscious. Brian climbed into the narrow hospital bed and held me until the morning.

JUNE 9, 2014

June 9. The worst day of my life. June 8 was the day that Michael lived. We had the triumph of birth and completing the pregnancy. We had the joy of meeting him, holding him, and sharing him with our family. It was a wonderful day.

On June 9, he was dead. We were in the hospital recovering after giving birth to a baby that died. Of all the heart wrenching things we had been through so far, that was my lowest point.

We asked to see Michael again in the morning and spent some time with him. The nurses checked on me. Then we had to meet with the bereavement coordinator to decide what to do with Michael's body. I wanted him cremated. I could not picture putting his body in a casket in the cold, lonely ground. I wanted him in an urn, at home with me. Babies belong at home, with their mothers, not in a cemetery. None of this had been arranged ahead of time since he came unexpectedly early. I felt blessed that God spared us from going through that anguish while I was pregnant.

We were able to go home that day. Michael was dead, and medically, I was doing okay so there was no reason to stay. It was time to truly say our final goodbye to Michael. My favorite nurse, Julie, brought Michael in wrapped in his blanket, and tried to be cheery. We held him and took a few more pictures with our camera—just the three of us. I cherish those photos and those special, private moments. We had arranged to have

Michael cremated with his blue baby blanket. We cut off about a third of the blanket for us to take home and hold. We said goodbye and Julie came back to take Michael away.

With that, he was gone. I am never going to see him or hold him in this lifetime. My heart bled inside of me. We sat in the empty hospital room and wept, hoping that if we shed enough tears, we could stop and pull ourselves together in some sort of respectable fashion.

The moment is still overwhelming to think about. I would give anything to go back to that point in time. It was so final. It still hurts. But while it is final on earth, I know and rejoice in the fact that I will see him again in heaven. Not only that, but he will be healthy! Praise God! What an amazing truth! And that is my reason for hope. No matter how hard my grief is here on earth, I know that someday my tears will be permanently wiped away. God promises that, "He will wipe every tear from their eyes. There will be no more death or mourning or crying or pain" (Revelation 21:4).

For some reason, I was given the option of walking to the car once we got off the labor and delivery unit. I wanted to walk, but I almost passed out waiting for the elevator and had to sit for a few minutes. Here I was again, already trying to act as if I was fine and everything was normal.

I called Mom as we drove home. She was still at the rehab facility recovering from her two broken legs. I told her we were probably going to have a funeral for Michael in a few weeks. Mom paused and said, "I don't think I will be able to do that." I was crestfallen. I told her I would arrange for her to have a wheelchair transport and a caregiver to attend to her, but again she said, "No, that won't work."

I was absolutely crushed. I started crying so hard, I was inconsolable. I felt like I lost Mom's support when she fell, and she was not even going to try to make it to my son's funeral. Later, Mom said she was operating out of fear, but it really hurt. I was so fragile. She was still gone from my life.

We drove home, and Brian pulled into the garage. We sat there a minute or two before getting out of the car. We were back at a familiar place, yet things had totally changed. I felt so different. The house felt empty. Constance was with Charlotte, or maybe Lynn—I don't even know who—but I knew she was safe and having fun. Brian and I wanted another night alone together.

It was strange to be home with nothing to do. Some of Brian's dad's friends had purchased dinner for us and put it in our fridge. While I was medically stable, I was physically and emotionally exhausted. We laid in bed and watched *Back to the Future*. Something familiar and lighthearted.

Night fell and we went to bed early. Brian fell asleep right away. Just like the night before, I closed my eyes and felt wide awake. Brian had to get up early for work the next day (his usual time—3:00 a.m.—*crazy, I know*) so I did not want to disturb his short slumber. I turned on the light in my closet, sat on the floor, and pulled out the binder that I had hidden away just a few months before. I read every piece of paper that I had received over the course of the pregnancy. I re-read all the doctor's notes. I read the information about trisomy 18 that I had been given by the genetic counselor that I was too afraid to look at.

For the first time, it all made sense. The trisomy 18 literature explained what to expect and the details of Michael's prognosis. It explained how slim his chances were for survival. At that very moment, it became clear—Michael never really had a chance. He was never going to be long in this world. I had not been able to see that while I was pregnant, and that was okay. I didn't need to. I needed to have the hope that maybe he would live. It was the only way I was able to survive our pregnancy.

As the hours passed, I realized I needed some sleeping medication. I dug through my hospital bag and pulled out the handwritten prescription for Ambien that I politely accepted from the nurse at the hospital. I was already on Vicodin and not supposed to drive, but I did not want to wake up Brian. The drugstore was only a quarter mile away. I drove there, teary-eyed, and walked to the back where the pharmacy was located.

Along the way, I ran into a sales clerk. She said hello, and I burst into tears. As she gave me a hug, I let myself go and wept in her arms. Comforting me, she said, "It's okay. Whatever it is, it can't be that bad." I couldn't even respond out loud. *Yes, this is an occasion where it actually is "that bad." My son died yesterday.*

I made it back to the pharmacy counter and slammed the prescription down. "I need some medication." I looked like hell. Thank goodness they filled the prescription quickly and without any questions. I returned home, took the Ambien, and went to bed. Brian didn't even know I had left.

CHAPTER SIX

After Michael

THE EARLY DAYS

I woke up alone the next morning. Brian had already left for work. Lynn brought Constance home later that morning, and I was so happy to see her. Our sweet, wonderful miracle of a daughter. Lynn gave me a hug, and I just held on to her and wept. Although it was really hard that my own mom was not around, I was grateful for Lynn.

Physically, I was very weak from giving birth and losing so much blood in the process. I was even further weakened by the tremendous emotional toll. I literally could not think. While I was happy to have Constance back at home, I was not capable of caring for her that day. I called my friend Alicia in a panic on that first full day home. Alicia is the most generous, giving person I know, without a doubt. She has her hands full caring for her disabled son, but she made arrangements and drove across town to help me.

I thought that the pregnancy—carrying a baby with a terminal diagnosis—was the hard part. I was way wrong. That was difficult, of course. And the miscarriages were emotional too. But the sorrow I felt from the miscarriages didn't even compare to the pain of losing a child. In retrospect, they seemed like mere bumps in the road compared to how I felt right after Michael died. I didn't understand why. His life was so short.

We were totally unprepared for Michael's birth and death. The first few weeks were painful and tender. It was so hard. Everything. Moving. Breathing. Eating. Thinking. Living. I was totally devastated and totally destroyed. My world had fallen apart.

I had told my boss that when Michael was born, I would need a leave of absence, regardless of the outcome. I planned to take six to eight weeks off and reevaluate from there.

Brian's job didn't allow for him to step away for any time at all. He owned a food distribution route in the grocery industry. Even though he was self-employed, or maybe because of that, his job was incredibly rigid and inflexible. His grocery store accounts needed to be seen, and there was no one else to do it. Brian was extremely supportive when he was around, but there were so many times that he was not there, and I felt alone. I wished Brian was able to take that first week off, but he had to go back to work.

One day in that first week, Constance and I were trying to get out the door to run a simple errand. She was being a typical three-year-old and not cooperating with my instructions to get in the car. Before I realized what I was doing, I slapped her. Both of us burst into tears—shocked at what I had just done. I had absolutely no reserves in my patience to handle her. I immediately called Charlotte and tearfully asked her if she could watch Constance until Brian came home. Without hesitating, she said yes, even though she had three young children of her own. That was what I needed, and that was best for Constance.

At first, I was afraid to be by myself all day. I didn't want to be with people, yet I needed help taking care of not just myself but also of Constance (I felt particularly bad about this). Shouldn't I spend all my time with her since I lost my son? Wouldn't that make me feel better? Well no, of course not. I had to take care of myself. Laura, from String of Pearls, always had such great advice. She had other children before she lost Pearl, and she said that kids recover. They will remember parts of it, but not all of it. And even if they sit in front of the TV all day for a while, that is okay! That helped relieve me of the guilt.

It was hard to recover at home without my mom around. If she was healthy, I knew she would have been over every single day, just like she was when Constance was born. But since she could not, I had to rely on other people. As good as my friends were, they were not the same as my own mom. I let people come over, and it was sort of helpful. At least it passed the time. Many people brought meals. It is amazing how a simple dinner could be so comforting.

We started getting cards and gifts about two days after we came home. I loved getting the mail every day, and I was touched by how many people sent cards. We got beautiful gifts—flowers, music, chocolate, mementos—from so many people. Old friends. New friends. Family friends. Friends of friends. Distant relatives. People we knew well and people we hardly knew at all. It validated my loss and made me feel not alone. I saved every card, and I read them over and over in the first year. Receiving all the support from others helped me heal from my other miscarriages too. Miscarriages are lonely. I grieved at the time, but I did not get the outpouring of support like I did when Michael died.

I visited Mom at the end of the first week. It was one of my first trips out of the house after Michael was born. As I pulled up to the rehab center, I remembered that the last time I was there, Michael was alive in my belly. Now he was not. I sat in the same recliner chair and talked with Mom. It all felt so different. I wondered if the nurses would notice I was no longer pregnant. They didn't. That was okay.

I missed Mom. Conversation was hard. There was a distance now. I could not be there for her, and she could not be there for me. My brother, Neil, came out from New York a couple of weeks later. As we sat on the patio at Mom's rehab, I thought about how broken my family seemed to be.

BREASTMILK

In addition to trying to heal physically from giving birth and emotionally from Michael's death, within a few days, my breastmilk came in. It seemed painfully cruel. I was full of milk with nowhere to expel it to relieve the engorgement. String of Pearls gave me some cream to help reduce the production, and I was advised to wear tight-fitting clothing to also suppress my supply. It was miserable. What a bitter reminder of our loss. I had milk to feed a baby, but no baby to care for. I knew I could donate to a milk bank, but that took energy that I did not have, and I just wanted it to go away. I felt bad for not helping other moms in need, but there is a time and place to help. This was not the time. Someone else could help.

I was angered by my milk supply, but like my grief, I could not ignore it. I had to accept that my body made it. It was the same with our loss. I wanted to discount the grief and believe that Michael's life didn't count because he lived for such a short time. That it was not a significant loss because we knew he was sick. None of that was true. Ultimately, I accepted the fact that my body was making milk for a dead baby. I embraced it as a sign of his life—that his life was real and it did matter. It "counted." After about three weeks, my supply dried up. I cried so hard when it was gone. Another sign that Michael's earthly life was over, and my milk truly wasn't needed.

READING AND RECOVERY

My routine in the early days consisted of waking up, having breakfast, and then sitting on my back deck. As I said at the beginning, we have a nice life in the boring suburbs. Our backyard is nice, but quite average. You can imagine it—a strip of grass, a view of the neighbor's house beyond the fence, and

mediocre landscaping that we tried to keep on top of. Despite
the botanical shortcomings of tract housing, it was a lovely time
of year. Everything was starting to become green and bloom.

Some of my memories from Michael's death are so vivid,
and others are like a fog. I don't remember where Constance
was in those early days, but I suppose she was at daycare. On
the mornings that I did not have Constance to care for, I sat
outside on my deck and read, prayed, and cried. So many tears
needed to come out, like when you need to blow your nose
after a bad sinus infection. They could not stay in, and it was a
relief to get them out.

In the box from String of Pearls—the one that I didn't have
the courage to open ahead of time—was a book called *A Gift
of Time: Continuing Your Pregnancy When Your Baby's Life
is Expected to Be Brief* by Amy Kuebelbeck and Deborah L.
Davis. It was a compilation of quotes and stories from a dozen
or so women who had gone through the same things as me.
The women spoke about what they went through during pregnancy, at doctor's appointments, after delivery, and after death.

While it would have been so helpful to have read it ahead
of time, I had been in survival mode and could not have
handled it. I devoured the four-hundred-page book—circling
and putting stars and double stars next to the comments that
rang true for me. I felt validated by reading near-identical
thoughts, struggles, and experiences of these other women.
There was another book in the box called *The One Year Book
of Hope Devotional* by Nancy Guthrie. Nancy had two babies,
separately, that both died of a genetic condition around six

months. The devotional book explored bringing our grief to a good and just God.

I also received a couple of books from my mom's cousin about loss—*Experiencing Grief* by H. Norman Wright and *Teardrop Diary* by Erin McSparron. I knew nothing about grief, and they helped me understand what I was feeling and why. I sat outside for hours in my backyard, communing with God. I read my books, I read the Bible, I journaled. I prayed. I wrote letters to Michael. I sat in the sunshine and stared at the blue sky. I felt the breeze and knew that God was very, very close. It was my Garden of Eden. I look back on those tender days of mourning and miss them. Not the grief, but how tangible God was. God's presence is one of the rich blessings of suffering.

As I sat outside and grieved, I worked out my emotions through applying God's Word into my situation. His Word washed over my broken heart and expressed my feelings for me. "Out of my distress I called on the Lord; the Lord answered me and set me free" (Psalm 118:5, RSV).

Different Bible passages jumped out at me as I read them through the lens of Michael's short life. The words brought me comfort. "This is what the Lord says—he who created you, Jacob, he who formed you, Israel: 'Do not fear, for I have redeemed you; I have summoned you by name; you are mine'" (Isaiah 43:1). As much as I loved Michael, I was reassured thinking about how even more precious he was to God, the creator of life. "I will bring your children from the east and gather you from the west...Bring my sons from afar and my daughters from the ends of the earth—everyone who is called by my name, whom I created for my glory, whom I formed and made" (Isaiah 43:5–7). God knew Michael before he was even born and called him to heaven for His glory.

In the evenings, when I couldn't grieve outside, I was drawn to Michael's room. It was such a blessing to have set up the nursery before Michael was born. We certainly would not have done it afterward, but it was wonderful to have a space that was dedicated to him—just as a living baby would need its own space. In the dark of the night and later in the coldness of winter, I sat in his room. I rocked in the rocking chair, holding his urn and blanket, just like how I would have rocked him to sleep if he were living. It was as close to him as I could physically get. We had a large photograph of the three of us set up across the room so I could look at him as I rocked. I looked at the pictures from his birth over and over and over again.

FUNERAL PLANNING

Before Michael was born, even when I could not imagine him dying, I knew I wanted a memorial service for him. So many people supported us on our journey, and I wanted to celebrate Michael's life with them. We did not get to do that for Daniel and Sarah.

Being unprepared for his early birth and death, we had to quickly select a mortuary for cremation before we left the hospital. I was familiar with funeral homes in the area since I worked with the elderly, but I did not know if one was better than another for a child. We had more time to select an urn. Charlotte helped by calling a few different funeral homes to find out who had a decent selection of infant urns.

It was important to me to get Michael's ashes back from the crematory and into an urn. My motherly instinct wanted him with me. We set up an appointment with a funeral director at a well-established home a week after Michael was born. Physically, I was still very weak. We were greeted by a man who looked young. I look young for my age (I am not sure how much longer I can get away with saying that!), but I have a lot of experience with the elderly and get frustrated that I have to prove my credibility. I did not want to judge our funeral director by his immature appearance either. However, it turned out my instincts were right.

His name was Andrew. He was awkward and insulting from the start, crudely asking how long Michael lived. He lacked compassion, and he seemed uncomfortable with my answer. He walked us into a showroom and helped us look through a catalog (while standing, I may add). We agreed pretty quickly on a beautiful silver moon. The two tips of the crescent touched to form a circle, and it had a profile of a face in it. It seemed whimsical and fitting for a baby.

I inquired about some jewelry that was on display. Andrew explained that you could put your loved one's ashes in it. However, he quickly steered me away from it because, "What if someone broke into your house and stole it?" I found that somewhat insulting—that I couldn't choose what I wanted, and he thought our house could be burglarized.

I asked him if we could sit down while we were completing the paperwork. A glass of water would have been nice, too, especially since we were making a purchase of several hundred dollars. *No, Andrew, don't trouble yourself.* Having never done this before, we asked how it worked. "Will the urn come to our house, and will we need to deliver it to you? Or will it go to the crematory where Michael's ashes are?" We simply didn't know, and they were reasonable questions.

Well, this clown responded, "Oh no. All the caskets and urns are loaded up on a big coffin truck. You wouldn't want that pulling up on your street!"

Finally it was time to pay. String of Pearls was wonderful and had offered to pay for Michael's urn. We explained this to Andrew and gave him the contact information. And as if to eliminate any doubt about what a jerk he was, he would not let us leave until he got ahold of Laura, the director from String of Pearls, to approve the charges. When he stepped out of the room to make the call, Constance said, "I don't like him." *Out of the mouth of babes!*

I was so mad at him. He was the most insensitive person I met during our entire loss experience. At first, I wasn't sure if I was oversensitive because we were grieving. But it hung with me. About six months later, I wrote a letter to the owner of the multi-location funeral home, and included the fact that I work with the elderly and refer business to them. The owner called me immediately to apologize. I wished I had complained in a timelier manner, but I was just trying to survive. I knew they were a good company. Andrew was just a seriously rotten egg.

MICHAEL'S SERVICE

Charlotte and Pastor Joe were instrumental in planning the funeral. Our church meets at a high school, so Charlotte found a church through another friend, who had lost two babies, that would let us use their sanctuary. Joe came up with an outline to guide us in the planning. It came together beautifully.

We had Michael's service on Saturday, June 28, about three weeks after Michael was born. While we were planning this, I was in survival mode, so I overlooked inviting some key people. My brother, Neil, had flown into town the week before, but I was not quite ready to have it then. One of my biggest regrets was that we did not pay for him to fly out to Colorado again for the service. There was so much of the experience of losing Michael that I just did not know how to handle. Brian's dad and stepmom flew out and so did one of Brian's brothers. It really was a family event, and not just a gathering of local friends. I wished I had put it on Facebook to get the word out so a few special friends could have come who prayed so faithfully for me throughout the pregnancy.

Despite Mom's initial hesitation, and with a few weeks of recovery behind her, she was able to come in a wheelchair with a four-hour pass from her doctor. I arranged for a trusted co-worker from the home care company to be her personal attendant.

Brian wore a suit, and I wore a dress that did not look half bad over my flabby stomach. Constance wore her Easter dress. As we got ready to leave the house, it struck me, *Wow, we are going to our son's funeral.* This was significant. I never envisioned ourselves in that situation, yet at the same time, I was excited for the opportunity to share with our friends and family.

The service was absolutely beautiful and about a hundred people attended. Like a proud mama, I wanted to share Michael's life with everyone. I also wanted to share our story and thank all the people who supported us for the last year.

We asked people to bring a small stone to symbolize each life that Michael touched. I love the stones—people brought all kinds—shells, glass, natural, polished, and ones with Bible verses written on them. They are in a large, shallow bowl on my dresser, and I see them every morning when I get dressed. At the service, I included a poem that I adapted and rearranged for Michael from *Teardrop Diary* by Erin McSparron. The poem is included at the end of this book.

Besides celebrating Michael's life, the funeral service also gave me an opportunity to mourn and celebrate the lives of Daniel and Sarah. Miscarriages feel so hidden and secretive. People were sympathetic once they heard about our miscarriages, but I had to let them know about them in the first place. It was healing to be able to publicly acknowledge all our losses.

I shared what I had learned so far from the pregnancy and in the first three weeks of recovery. I shared how I felt a connection to Mary, Jesus' mother, who also had a son who died. I shared how Michael was our little visitor, who briefly came into this world before departing for eternity in heaven. And most importantly, I tried to share our love for him with those who supported us.

I ended by reading this letter to Michael which I had written in the first week after he died:

Dear Michael,

My sweet baby Michael. How I miss you and love you. How I long to hold you again. Those precious moments at the hospital were too short. I am so grateful for you—grateful that God intentionally gave you to us to be your parents.

Losing Daniel was a shock and I was afraid to get to know Sarah out of fear of losing her too. But after those miscarriages I learned to embrace life over fear—it didn't protect me from the pain anyway. I learned what it feels like to have a life inside of me long before there are outward signs of pregnancy. I know what it is like because I know the empty feeling when it is gone.

After losing Sarah I was filled with great hope—hope that the next time would be different! And it was different with you. Because of what I learned from the miscarriages, I was able to get to know you the moment you were created. I carried you for seven months and you were—and are—a member of our family. Constance played with you every day, shared toys with you, tickled you, kissed you and talked to you. You kicked me, poked me, and pushed on me so I could never forget that you were there.

Michael, I rejoice in the gift of your life. I rejoice that we were able to carry you and give you 20 minutes on earth. I thank God that He gave us the gift of meeting you and holding you before you left us. Oh Michael, you were so beautiful—not deformed like how the doctors portrayed you to be. You came suddenly and unexpectedly, but it was your time. As Paul says in Ephesians, "For we are God's handiwork, created in Christ Jesus to do good works" (Ephesians 2:10). God ordained the time for you to come because it was time for you to go.

Your sweet body was warm and beautiful. Holding you was one of the best moments of my life. And by God's grace you opened your eyes for a brief moment before you died.

Oh Michael, I want you back. But you were sick. God had a plan and a purpose for you. I am grateful that He used me and Brian in that plan. We prayed for a miracle but held our hands out to God to give and receive whatever He had planned. I'm grateful for His abounding goodness, mercy and love—all of which we feel so clearly in our lives.

You are our gift and undoubtedly worth all the nausea, exhaustion, uncertainty, sorrow and anguish—worth it to meet you and know you. Life truly is a precious gift no matter how short it is.

I love you Michael and give your life to the Lord.
Love, Mom

Brian shared without prepared notes, and it was great. He shared that God the Father said to Jesus, "'You are my Son, whom I love; with you I am well pleased'" (Mark 1:11). God said this to Jesus before He died on the cross and before He even started his ministry on earth. God simply loved Him because He was His Son.

We also gave Brian's parents and my dad the chance to briefly share what Michael's life meant to them. Dad said Michael was our shooting star who briefly lit up our life. Lynn shared how her love for Michael was intensified, not weakened, in the short period of time that she had with him.

So many people came up to us after the service with tears streaming down their faces and thanked us for sharing. A former neighbor was there, and she told me that she was going directly to Presbyterian St. Luke's hospital after the funeral to visit Jenny, an old classmate of mine, who had just lost her baby named Callan the day before. I was sad to hear that someone I knew was going through the same experience that I was going through.

We had a potluck reception after that. Mom was able to stay, which was nice. The whole day felt surreal. By the afternoon, I was exhausted. I said goodbye to my in-laws who had flown into town, and I went to bed for the rest of the day.

STUMBLING THROUGH THE FIRST MONTH

Planning and anticipating the funeral took a major part of my focus the first few weeks. Since I had not experienced the death of a significant loved one before this, I expected to feel better after the funeral. I expected to be done with this chapter in my life. There were many more times after this that I expected to be "done." After delivery, after the funeral, after maternity leave. It took me a long time just to accept that I would not be "done" on my timeline and even longer to understand why. I expected to be done grieving after Michael's first birthday. Now I am glad that I am not "done." Michael is my son, and his death has changed my outlook on life. I think of him daily.

As the enormity of our loss unfolded before me, I struggled when I realized that part of me would always be sad. I wanted to "get over it," like how one heals from a scraped knee. I truly expected life would reset to normal. I read that life would never go back to how it was, but instead there would be a "new normal." I hated that. That was not what I wanted. Life before Michael was fine. I didn't want to be sad. I didn't want my life to be changed. I wanted this horrible part of our life to be over and forgotten. But now, a few years later, that sadness has transformed into a beautiful memory of an experience that I would not give up.

So understandably, I was surprised that I was still sad the day after the funeral. We had not been to church since before Michael was born. We went the day after the service, and in hindsight, I wished we had not. One service was enough for the weekend. But Brian poorly reasoned that sooner or later, we would have to go, so let's get it over with. Now we both know better.

Being around other people was really, really hard. While people at our church, like any good church, are kind, loving, and genuine, you still put on a polite smile. I did not have a smile in me, yet I felt forced to produce one. As nice as everyone was, church was still a crowd. Being around a group of people was the last thing I wanted to do. I took Constance back to her Sunday school class. I could barely make eye contact with anyone. I felt so raw.

There was a very nice new family dropping off their son at Sunday school. They were close to our age and had a boy who was Constance's age. They seemed like people we would have been friends with under other circumstances. The husband, Tim, was going to be a new associate pastor, and this was their first Sunday attending our church. I could not muster up any energy to even greet them. The wife, Michelle, innocently said "Hi" to me, like it was any normal Sunday. *We just celebrated the death of my son. Why don't you know that?* I managed to mumble "Hi" back.

GRIEVING AS A FAMILY

Besides feeling raw as an individual in those first few weeks, the loss was challenging for us as a married couple and as a family. I felt alone; Brian didn't know how to support me or how to express what he was feeling as he grieved. We often were short with each other in the early months. Having no reserves to show each other grace, sensitive feelings were easily trampled on. Constance, picking up on our heartache, and also grieving in her own little way, was much more emotional than normal. She cried more easily and seemed to throw more fits than I could handle. We were a mess, just as any family in this situation would be. Everything felt like a struggle.

But in the end, we overcame our hurts and were there for each other. The best thing we did was to strip away all the distractions and just simply be with each other. Making time to listen to each other, to hold each other while we cried, and just to sit together were the most comforting things that we did, which enabled us to stumble our way through the loss and come out still intact on the other side. Now we are a stronger unit—like having gone through a refiner's fire. But it was difficult, and I can see how stress from the death of a child can lead to divorce. Very easily. We started with such a strong foundation, and it still tested our limit.

SUMMER

The summer continued. My maternity leave was such a tender, precious time. I continued my routine of sitting outside, reading, and crying every morning. Sometimes it was for twenty minutes, and sometimes it was for a few hours. I watched the trees, felt the cool breeze, and the warm sun. I figured I was probably going to get skin cancer, but that did not matter to me at the time. *(Three years later, I did. Basal cell carcinoma on my forehead. Wear sunscreen, people!)* I watched the butterflies flutter through our yard. I journaled. I prayed. In the evenings, I sat in Michael's room, looking at his pictures, crying, and holding his urn while rocking him to sleep and saying goodnight, just as any mother of a newborn would do.

String of Pearls continued to support me. They had their annual 5K run about six weeks after Michael was born. I had not worked out at all since Michael was born, but I was determined to do the run. With my belly jiggling, I ran about two and a half miles and walked the final leg. I was pretty proud of it. The finish line of the race was lined with signs with the names of all the String of Pearls babies. I noticed that Michael's sign was next to the sign for a baby named Callan, the son of my former high school classmate. I took a picture of it to show her if we ever reconnected.

So many people and moms were at this event. Did this many people really lose babies and survive the experience? Everyone was so kind. It was quite moving for me, and needless to say, I was physically and emotionally spent for the rest of the day.

BABYMOON: FUTURE PLANS

Michael was scheduled to be born at the end of August. Some friends had previously given us a gift certificate for a weekend in Steamboat Springs, a mountain resort town, which we had planned to use for a babymoon in July. Since Michael was born two months early, our babymoon turned into a well-timed getaway for Brian and me to spend time alone together. I hoped to escape my grief for a weekend but was surprised to find that my emotions followed me. Despite being in a beautiful place with my wonderful husband, my grief was ever-present—it was the backdrop to everything I did. We had a good time—we slept in, hiked, ate out, and went to the hot springs—but I was still sad.

My favorite part of the weekend was Saturday afternoon. We bought a six-pack and sat along the bank of the river that ran through town. We drank our beer and daydreamed about the future, which led me to explore a dream that I had had for a while. For several years, I had wanted to start a geriatric care management practice, but it was always just an idea. The thought of going out on my own was scary. *I can't work for myself, let alone run my own business.*

But as we sat by the Yampa River, I was free to dream about what I would call my company, what services I would offer, and how I would get started. That weekend, Kinsman Care Management, LLC was born. Afterward, I wrote down what we talked about and set it aside. While I was excited about the idea, I was still on maternity leave and did not feel like I was in a place to start something new. I just wanted to go back to the security of my job of four-plus years, which I knew inside and out.

THE JOHNSONS

We returned home from our babymoon and continued to put the pieces of our life back together. As I mentioned, Tim and Michelle Johnson were the new couple who joined the church the Sunday after Michael's funeral. Tim was going to be a new associate pastor. Pastor Joe encouraged us to get to know them. Even though I was freshly grieving, I felt an expectation to be hospitable. *That was dumb.* Michelle said that it was hard to take her three-year-old boy out to a restaurant, which I could understand. And since they were the new couple, it did not seem right for them to have us over. I felt a self-imposed obligation to invite them over to dinner. It was awful. It took so much out of me to prepare dinner that night—effort and energy that I didn't have.

Looking back on it, I both laugh and cringe, thinking about how preposterous it was to try to host people just a month or so after Michael's birth. I put myself in a position to give when I had absolutely nothing to give. Over and over during our string of losses, I did not give myself permission to just be—but no one else did either. Just as I was so greatly compromised by my grief, I was also greatly limited in my ability to self-assess. I had no insight into how much I was suffering. And while I had so many people caring for me, no one truly came forward to show me how to care for myself.

While the evening itself turned out fine, it made me resentful toward them, through no fault of their own. I wish I had enough insight to have simply said, "We would like to get to know you, but our son just died, and we can't host. Let's go out to Chick-fil-A." They would have understood. Or heck—here's a crazy thought—not do anything with them at all and let other church members welcome them. This is one of many things I would do over ... *Maybe someone can read this and learn from my errors.* I am sorry for the way I handled it and that it got our friendship off on the wrong foot, which continued to be a problem in the months to come.

RETURNING TO WORK

The summer went on, and it was time to think about returning to work. I was not sure how long a maternity leave I would take. There was not an infant that I needed to care for, but I knew I still needed time to heal. After about six weeks, I started to feel moments of normalcy creep back into my life. I felt like getting dressed in the morning. Taking a shower was no longer a major accomplishment for the day. It was actually fun to go to the playground with Constance again. I felt like I could start taking baby steps in our new life, rather than crawling through it.

My boss had a vacation planned in August, and I did not want to come back while he was gone—I knew better than that, based on when he went out of town in June! I should have taken two extra weeks and returned after his trip, but instead, like a perpetual overachiever to the point of my own detriment, I returned to work the week before he went out of town. An extra two weeks would have been good, and in the grand scheme of things, not that big of a deal. *Why do I make things harder than they need to be?*

I gathered the strength to get dressed up and nervously drove to work the morning of my return. Walking through the door of our office and facing my co-workers felt like climbing a mountain. As I crossed the office threshold, one of my co-workers jumped up, gave me a hug, and asked me how I was doing. Unexpectedly, I burst into tears. *Apparently, not so good.*

My desk was covered with cards and small gifts from my co-workers and other marketing people in the industry. It was wonderful. I simply sat at my desk the first week I was back and stared at the wall. After a few days, my office mate gently asked, "Are you going to go out and do marketing?" That was, after all, my primary job responsibility. "Eventually," I replied.

I was scared to leave the security of our office. I did not want to put on a smile and ask people for their business. My baby was dead. Drumming up referrals for home care was inconsequential. But I had to do it. It wasn't pretty. I started with my easy accounts—the people who knew me and whom I considered friends on some level. Next, I went to hospice companies because that's what they did—cared for people in the midst of a death. Finally, I took marketing material to places where I was able to just drop it off and didn't have to interact with anyone.

I felt different. I had been changed. There were people I called on who did not know I just had a baby. As I gave them my pitch for why they should use our home care company, I thought in the back of my head, *You have no idea what I just went through. How can we be talking about this?* I avoided networking groups for a while. Those were the worst—a group of cheery marketing people with whom you had to mingle and make small talk.

I finally went to an open house party at an assisted living community in October. As I walked into the crowded room, I thought I was ready. At first, it was nice to see some of my marketing friends. But then I reached my limit. It came on quickly. Over and over, people asked, "How are you?" Or, "How was your summer?" There was no good answer to any of these questions. I could only share so many times about Michael, or not share and pretend that I had a good summer, all the while thinking about how tragic it was. I could no longer hold in my tears. I panicked—the room suddenly felt cramped. I pushed through the crowd to get to the door.

As I was trying to leave, a friend stopped me and said, "Hi, I would like to introduce you to someone." The other woman turned around to reveal she was at least seven months pregnant. I felt like I was in a horror movie when the clown turns around in slow motion to reveal that he is the maniacal killer. I threw my business card at her and exclaimed, "Sorry, I gotta go!" My wound was still so sensitive that even just seeing a pregnant woman evoked powerful feelings of sorrow. It was painful.

But I made it. Like starting to do marketing again, I got through it.

One of the worst parts was interacting with all the people who knew I had my baby. Some knew we were expecting some sort of difficulty, so in that respect, I was glad that I had told some people ahead of time that there would be a problem.

Some only saw I was pregnant beforehand and now I was not, so they understandably concluded that I had a healthy baby. Those people were the hardest to deal with. It was so difficult handling their innocent comments. "You had your baby! Congratulations." *Yes, he's dead.* If I was truthful, then they felt horrible. If I pretended to go along with their comments, then I felt even worse and alone in my grief. Plus, then they would follow up with all the wrong questions: "How does Constance like being a big sister?" "How's he eating?" "Who watches him?"

There were times that dark humor was the only way I could cope. "Oh, you've had your baby! What's he like?" *Really quiet!*

"Is he sleeping through the night?" *Yep, since day one!*

Sometimes, I got tired of the unintentionally hurtful questions and gave them a delightfully direct answer. "How is your baby doing?" "Oh, he's dead." Now, I didn't always say that. I had my canned answer that I had to give so many times. "He had some health problems, and he died shortly after birth. We are grateful to have met him." That was the most simple and sincere answer, but just blurting out he was dead and seeing the look of horror on the other person's face was pretty refreshing now and then. They could handle a moment of pain after what I had been through.

SUPPORT GROUP

Laura, from String of Pearls, let us know about an upcoming six-week support group for parents who had lost babies through stillborn birth or neonatal death. I called the organizer to see if we could participate. I explained that we had two miscarriages and a neonatal death within an eighteen-month period. "Does that meet your criteria?" I nervously asked, still afraid that Michael's life didn't count, that my grief wasn't valid, and therefore my experience would be rejected. Somewhat taken aback by the amount of loss in a short period of time, she said, "Yes!" in a startled but sympathetic voice.

We showed up for the first meeting in August, not knowing what to expect and trying to guard our fragile emotions. We joined another couple, a single woman, and the facilitator, Kim

Woods. Moments later, my old high school acquaintance Jenny (whom my former neighbor visited after Michael's funeral) walked in with her husband, Matt. I immediately stood up, and we embraced each other in the middle of the room. It was so nice to see an old friend with whom I now felt so intimately connected. Her husband had no idea who I was and later told Jenny that he figured that everyone in the group was supposed to hug like that!

The first session consisted of everyone telling their story. For all seven of us participants, it was our first time sharing our story from the beginning to the present, and also the first time hearing the painful, yet similar stories of others who were newly in the same shoes. Kim, our facilitator, started. She had three miscarriages and then a stillborn baby, Caleb, who passed away from an umbilical cord accident one day prior to being induced.

Another couple, Mike and Erin, had a baby, Owen, with a congenital heart defect. They were unaware of his condition prior to his birth; he died twelve hours later. Erin, a high school teacher, gave birth to Owen on a Friday. The school joyfully announced his arrival leading into the weekend. On Monday, the school had to make a second announcement with the devastating news. We shared our story next. It was so good to patch our experience together into a timeline and say the words of our story out loud. Then Matt and Jenny shared their story. Their baby, Callan, had hydrocephalus and was born at the end of June, the day before Michael's funeral. She did not find out there was a problem until she was thirty-two weeks along. Callan lived about seven hours.

The final story was from Nari, an unmarried Japanese woman. She had lived in the United States for about five years. She had a boyfriend, and they found out their baby had trisomy 18, like us, around twelve weeks. Her boyfriend wanted her to abort, but she did not want to do that. He broke up with her, and she carried her terminal pregnancy alone. She had her baby girl, Mizuki, which means moonlight in Japanese, just three weeks before our first meeting. Losing Michael was hard enough, but I could not fathom doing it without a partner. We were heartbroken upon hearing her story. We were in awe that she managed to get herself dressed to come to this meeting so soon after birth.

Our first meeting went an hour over the allotted time. It was so healing, so wonderful, yet so intense. We all cried listening to each other's stories—simultaneously grieving for our own babies and the ones we were just hearing about. It was powerful to connect with others who had just gone through similar traumatic experiences. Kim wrapped up our meeting by letting us know about "grief hangovers." After sharing such intense stories, she said we may want to be a little easy on ourselves tomorrow. And of course—true to form—I completely ignored her advice and planned to have a normal day.

The next morning, I could barely get out of bed. I dragged myself to work and sat at my desk, staring at the dull, gray wall three feet in front of me for most of the morning. I talked to my office mate, I shuffled papers on my desk, I touched the keys of my laptop—I went through the motions of working. Again and again, I ask myself, *Why didn't I just take the day off?* Trying to work that day was totally pointless. I just wanted to be "all better."

The rest of our support group sessions were wonderfully helpful. We checked in each time about how our week had been. We talked about the five stages of grief and that they are not really "stages" at all. We brought in photos and shared precious mementos of our babies. Unfortunately, Nari only came for one more session. She said that it was too hard to be around people, but she was glad she shared and heard our stories. She eventually moved back to New York to be closer to her sister, which I was glad to hear. I think about her and hope she is doing well.

By the end of six sessions, I was ready for the group to end. The group helped me start to accept our loss, but its short-term nature also served a purpose. I could see how an ongoing group could easily turn from a productive time of grieving to a pity party. There is a time for everything, and I was ready to move forward as I continued to process my grief.

RUNNING GROUP

Jenny, my new old friend, told me that she and another woman I knew from high school were starting to run together on Sunday mornings. Having a significant amount of baby weight to lose, that sounded great. We have run together every Sunday (weather and travel plans permitting) since then. *Can I still claim that it's "baby weight" that I need to lose?!* I cherish our friendship that has grown over these last few years and the opportunity to check in with each other every week about our grief.

Interestingly, Jenny hovers somewhere between an atheist and agnostic. I especially appreciate our friendship in light of our different beliefs. We have a very open friendship, and I feel comfortable sharing how my faith shapes my grief, just as she feels free to share how she is grieving in the absence of faith in a higher power. Our other friend, Annie, had struggled with years of infertility and was still on her journey to motherhood. No topic was off-limits in our weekly, four-mile conversation. Our friendship has grown beyond just talking about grief and loss, and I am grateful I can count on Jenny and Annie every week to share how things are going.

Having another mother who was going through the same experiences as I was going through, at the same time, was so affirming. And our conversations were not all sad, either. As Proverbs 17:22 says, "A cheerful heart is good medicine, but a crushed spirit dries up the bones." Only with each other could we share morbid humor to blow off some of the unknowingly insensitive comments that other people would say to us during the week. It became a wonderful joke between us to replay painful exchanges from the week with more satisfying answers. "How is your baby sleeping?" "He's a great sleeper. *Really* quiet!"

JOYFUL MOMENTS

The first four months after Michael was born were tender, but they weren't filled with sadness all the time. God gave us some bright spots that were truly special. For a long time, feeling happy was foreign to me. We went to a wedding at the end of

July at the same church where we were married. It was refreshing to have a happy event to get dressed up for and to think about our wedding day. I even managed to find an outfit that looked somewhat good on my post-baby body. The big difference now was that we had an adorable three-year-old with us who could really cut a rug! And she made sure not to let me and Brian dance without her! It felt good to have a break from feeling sad.

One of the joys of parenthood is that you get to re-experience all the fun things from childhood through your child's eyes. For Halloween, we decided to dress up as Mary Poppins and Bert, and Constance joined in to be Jane. It felt good to have a lighthearted project to work on together as a family. The costumes turned out great, and Halloween was another fun night for us.

BABY SHOWER

I had heard that other mothers who lose babies do not go to baby showers ever again. I was determined not to let our loss affect how I interacted with others—especially other friends and pregnant people. It didn't feel right that just because we had something sad happen to us that I shouldn't be happy for other people's pregnancies. Well, that was a big fat falsehood. It's totally reasonable that I wasn't happy for them. They don't need me. Let all the other people be happy for them.

That September, my dear friend Alicia was having her second baby, and a mutual best friend was throwing a shower for her. I have been friends with her since middle school, and I wanted to show my support, so I made plans to go. *Stupid.*

The day of the shower arrived. I brought Mom with me, both because she was invited and as my personal crutch. I mingled around the room and tried to be "the old normal." I felt weird talking to people. My head felt like it was floating, and I could not put an intelligible sentence together. I planned to stay just long enough to say hello. As I headed for the door to leave, the host announced they were gathering for a time of prayer and sharing. *Okay, I'll stick around for that.* I didn't pray, but I did pretty good with the listening.

However, that led right into opening presents and cooing over adorable little baby clothes. Suddenly, I had had enough. The walls started closing in. My enormous, eight-month pregnant friend was blocking the entire door in the small living room. What's more, my mom was not sitting next to me, and there was no way to subtly get her attention to slip out. So I just sat there, trying not to cry and ruin her shower. I left the second the ladies got up and cried with my mom all the way home. In hindsight, it was pretty clear I shouldn't have gone. I eventually made it to another baby shower five years later and it was still a rough experience.

FIRST PREGNANCY AFTER MICHAEL

We settled into our rhythm for the fall. Constance started preschool. Brian and I worked during the week and went to church on Sundays after I exercised with my running group. We started hosting a small-group Bible study at our house.

One Sunday evening, we were having dinner at Lynn's house. Just to make conversation, she casually mentioned that she heard that the associate pastor's wife, Michelle, was expecting. The news hit me hard. I fought back the tears. Lynn said she found out because Michelle told another woman at church who had been praying for her. She was the first person I knew who was pregnant after I lost Michael. I cried myself to sleep that night. I was jealous, and I felt the weight of our loss again—*Why did we lose Michael? Why couldn't we have another baby?*

Later that week, Michelle emailed me to see if I wanted to go out to coffee. I said yes and went along with it as if I didn't know why. We made some small talk, and finally she told me she was pregnant. I felt obligated to say, "I am happy for you but sad for me." But I wasn't happy for her. I wish I had allowed myself to be honest. Michelle is a caring person and could have handled it. After all, it was *really* thoughtful of her to recognize this would be hard and to take time to tell me personally.

I falsely put the expectation on myself that the right thing— the "Christian" thing—was to say I was happy for her. I wasn't. My reaction put an additional strain on our friendship with the Johnsons. I think the better response would have been to be authentic with my feelings and give myself permission to work those feelings out, rather than to sweep them under the rug. God does not ask us to hide our hurts, but rather to share them with others so we can be comforted.

ANTIDEPRESSANT

By then, it was October. I was surprised at how sad I still felt and that I couldn't just shake off those feelings. The sadness permeated me. In my self-imposed timeline of healing, I expected to be "better" by then. I decided to explore taking an antidepressant.

When I had left the hospital in June, they offered me a prescription for an antidepressant, which I initially turned down. I had never been on an antidepressant and did not think I would need it. I would rely on God; I would pray and I would heal. While still in the hospital, Becky, one of the nurses from String of Pearls, said that the medication can help with the range of emotions one may feel after a loss like this. At the time, I thought, *I made it through the pregnancy, isn't the hardest part over?*

Even in July, I had turned down Dr. Ziernicki's suggestion for trying Zoloft. I saw her, my original OB-GYN, for my six-week post-partum appointment. I had not seen her since our sixteen-week appointment when we decided to switch to DRS for prenatal care (although we had talked on the phone a few times). Seeing her was like being reunited with an old friend. She genuinely wanted to know how I was doing. I told her that it was still hard. She suggested trying Zoloft, but I didn't think I needed it.

About four months later, I was ready to reconsider my stance on antidepressants. I did not want someone to just pick a drug and have me try it to see how it affected me. I Googled "psychiatrists" and made a few calls to find someone who was taking new outpatient clients. Dr. Rachel Norwood was my gal.

I was nervous as I drove to my first appointment. *A psychiatrist?* People talk about how there shouldn't be a mental health stigma, but suddenly I felt self-conscious that it somehow applied to me. *I'm not mentally ill.* I waited in a small lobby. Dr. Norwood popped her head out and ushered me into a comfortable office, typically decorated with bookshelves full of self-help books, office plants, and a couch. She opened up the session by warmly asking, "Why do you want to go on antidepressant medication?"

When I had initially set up the appointment, I told her over the phone that I'd had some pregnancy losses and was still having a hard time with it. When we met in person, I gave more detail about my losses—two miscarriages in one year, followed by carrying a terminal pregnancy, and a neonatal death. As I finished telling her my story, she just sat there, dumbfounded. Her eyes grew wide. "You have been through so much." Her empathy really struck me and validated that what I had gone through was significant. I felt so alone in this. I barely knew any peers who'd had a miscarriage, let alone multiple ones.

Dr. Norwood explained how trauma after trauma builds on each other. She asked questions about how I was feeling. I told her I did not enjoy things I normally did, like cooking, and I was having a hard time concentrating—to the point that I couldn't even follow a recipe. She explained that an antidepressant doesn't take away the grief, but it can provide emotional scaffolding so the ups and downs of grief are not so severe. It lifts the cloud of sadness so one can think and process the loss. I liked that idea. Needless to say, I left with a prescription for Lexapro in my hand.

With caution, I started taking it. It was helpful, and I ended up taking it for about ten months. I stopped the summer after

Michael's first birthday. I kept hoping I was "done" and didn't need it anymore. I kept declaring it so. But of course, I couldn't declare it away. Dr. Norwood also explained how significant the first year was after a major loss. She said you have to get through the year of "firsts." The first holiday, the first time to the doctor, the first vacation, the first etc. I was grateful that I had my scaffolding that winter and spring …

THE HOLIDAYS

Fall turned colder, and the holidays descended upon us. All the books that I read and our support group stated how hard the holidays were after a loss. I did not understand why that would be. After all, Michael never lived during the holidays, so why would I miss him more? However, I did not understand or anticipate any of the grief that I was experiencing, so I decided to take their word for it. And they were right.

The holidays are hectic, stressful, and busy. Grieving makes it even harder to handle the busyness of life. Christmas was supposed to be a time of joy and celebration—which makes one's grief feel even more pronounced when one just can't come around to feel happy. And the holidays are also a time to be with loved ones—which makes one miss those who are gone even more. Especially sweet baby Michael, who I held for only twenty minutes, who never experienced a Christmas with us. This time the year before, we were newly pregnant, trying not to worry, and hoping for the best.

Anticipating and celebrating the birth of our newborn King triggered an emotional connection for me. All the stories about Mary and even Elizabeth and the images of Mary, blissfully holding her newborn Miracle, reminded me of Michael in a powerful way. It was hard to have that reminder, but also beautiful. As I said during the funeral, losing Michael gave me a stronger connection to Mary, knowing that she lost her son too. When I see Mary holding baby Jesus, I remember holding Michael on earth and also knowing that now Jesus is holding him in heaven.

Heeding advice, we tried to anticipate a difficult season it by making it simple. When I was single, I loved Christmas with all of its bustle and excitement. But when Brian and I got married, the responsibility of shopping, sending out cards, decorating, and who knows what else, all fell on me. That year we decided to keep it simple and include certain aspects we enjoyed and forego the rest. We let our family and friends know that we were skipping gifts, except for the children, and we kept our holiday outings to a minimum.

We went to one Christmas party with friends from church, but I really just went for Brian's sake. I hated it. I did not feel merry, and I did not want to make small talk or even try to come up with a socially appropriate answer to, "How are you?" *My heart is broken. How is your Christmas shopping going?* I stuck to grazing off the food table and hanging out with the children. They did not try to make small talk, and we made a killer house out of Legos.

One day during the Christmas season, we pulled out our decorations—one of my favorite parts of Christmas. I found our stockings and hung them up. But now there was one missing. I started to cry. We pledged to get one for Michael. We never quite made it to the store that year, but he has one now that we hang, and it feels right—he is our son, after all.

Brian, the most wonderful husband I could possibly have, bought me a ring for Christmas and gave it to me a few days early. A beautiful silver ring with a large, smoky quartz stone. I love it and wear it daily. Yes, it was an earthly treasure, but a big sparkly rock definitely brought some joy into the season! Later, I found out that smoky quartz is an alternative birthstone for June. It was an amazing coincidence, or was it?

The holidays came and went. We survived.

THE BIRTH OF KINSMAN CARE MANAGEMENT

After the initial adjustment of returning to work, I settled back into my old routine. I liked the company I worked for and had a lot of seniority. We were a small home care company that grew significantly while I worked there, and I had a lot of input on the overall operations. However, I had been there for over four years and was ready for another challenge.

For a while, I was grateful for its stability while I had so many losses on the personal side, but I was getting restless. I talked to my husband about it being time to quit and start my geriatric care management practice. *Is it crazy for me to start a company within the first year of my loss?* I knew it was, but I wanted to give it a try. I was good friends with my boss, the owner of the company, and I did not want my leaving to pose a hardship. I told him at the end of November that I was planning on leaving, and we worked on my transition for some time in the first quarter of the new year.

Leaving work was so much harder than I anticipated. I was 100 percent confident that it was what I wanted to do, but moving on from my old job was another loss, and I was so much more sensitive to that. I cried so hard on my last day. I was embarrassed. I hate when my emotions are stronger than my will.

My last day was Friday, January 30. I woke up the following Monday, unemployed and excited to get started on my new venture. I had taken some preliminary steps to establish my business, but I had more work to do before I could start taking on clients. Being in God's will is an exciting place to be, especially when His will calls you out of your comfort zone. It was so much fun to create my own brand. I poured myself into it, just like a mother pours herself into caring for a baby. Kinsman Care Management was my baby. And a very healthy one, indeed. I enjoyed creating a website, designing my logo, and setting up the foundational business operations. I vacillated between feeling the thrill of being on a roller coaster ride and the terror that my seatbelt may stop functioning at any moment. It was exhilarating to do something I never thought I would be capable of doing.

I opened my care management doors for business in March. I was excited to get my business off the ground and show off my new baby. Spreading the word was easy for me since I had been working in marketing for the past five years. I simply had to redefine my role as a geriatric care manager to all my contacts. Within a few weeks, I had several wonderful clients!

CONSTANCE HOSPITALIZED!

While my baby company was doing well, Constance was not. She had a typical little kid runny-nose cold in January and missed a day or two of daycare. She developed a nasty cough on the first full weekend in February. She did not sleep well at all Saturday night.

On Sunday, February 8, Brian had to merchandize his stores after church (yes—in the grocery business, you have to work seven days a week—*yuck!*), so I was home with Constance after my run. As we did the handoff, my dear husband naively said, "I think she is getting better." She had a coughing fit around 10:00 a.m. and fell asleep at 11:00 a.m. for an hour or so. When she woke up, she had a temperature of 103°F. She kept coughing but couldn't quite seem to get it all out.

This being a Sunday, her doctor's office was closed, but I felt she was too sick to wait another day. I thought maybe we could go to urgent care, and they could give her some antibiotics. I called Brian. No answer—his phone was probably still on mute from church. I loaded her in the car and drove to urgent care. After waiting a bit in the lobby, they called us back. They checked her temperature and oxygen level. It was 88 percent. I knew nothing about oxygen levels at that time. They told me that since she was having trouble breathing, she needed to go to a pediatric ER. *WHAT? My child can't breathe?* I called Brian. He still didn't answer. I frantically left Brian a message, "Urgent care said Constance is too sick. I am taking her to the ER. CALL ME!"

There were two pediatric hospitals in Denver: Children's Hospital and Rocky Mountain Hospital for Children, which is part of Presbyterian St. Luke's, where Michael was born. I drove Constance to Children's Hospital. I thought about how wonderful care was at Rocky Mountain Hospital for Children, but there was no way I was going back there.

I pulled up to Children's Hospital and brought Constance in. It was like entering a third-world country. The waiting room was packed—almost all the chairs were full of parents and children from all different nationalities and backgrounds. A distressed father, holding a young girl who was passed out in his arms, told the tech he was leaving to go to another hospital. I told the clerk who was checking people in that Constance had an oxygen saturation level of 88 percent. *Surely, they would triage her as a priority if she couldn't breathe, right?* They told me to sit in the lobby and wait with the rest of the people. I think if I dumbed it down and said my child can't breathe, they would have pulled out a nurse to check her.

As we sat and waited, with Constance burning up with her fever, I called Rocky Mountain Hospital for Children. They said there was only a five-minute wait. It was a twenty-five-minute drive, but that certainly would be quicker than where we were. I called Brian. Finally he answered. He was shocked to hear how sick she was. We decided that I would wait for him where I was, so we could drive to PSL together. There was no way I could do it alone.

I was so relieved to see him. The drive over felt surreal. Michael would have been eight-months old that very day. *Were we really driving over to the same place where Michael lived and died, now with another child?* I did not think Constance's illness was life-threatening, but returning to the hospital triggered vivid memories that made it hard not to worry about her.

The waiting room was empty. We got checked in, I told them my daughter had low oxygen levels, and we waited for a medical person to call us back to a room. Another family came in and was ushered back immediately.

"Why did they go back first?" I asked with my mama bear instincts coming out.

The clerk said, "He was having breathing problems." *Bingo—the magic password.*

Finally, we were put in a room, and she got medical attention. They immediately put oxygen on her, did a chest X-ray, and gave her a breathing treatment. Fortunately, she didn't have the flu or pneumonia, but she did have RSV—a common respiratory virus that is more serious in younger children.

"We'll get you moved upstairs as soon as we can," the doctor said to us.

"What!?" we asked. "Can't we go home?"

"No, with her oxygen level so low, she is too sick to go home. You'll stay the night here."

I was shocked. I am a well-educated person and an attentive mother, but in this case, I had no idea how sick she was. She was not blue or gasping for air (thank goodness!). The nurse showed me how her neck and stomach were contracting in an effort to get enough air.

We ended up staying in the hospital for three days and two nights, which was exhausting for all of us. We could have stayed a third night for additional observation, but we were ready to go home. They monitored her breathing, and she was on oxygen continuously. The staff was very nice, and Constance did great. In my book, she was the cutest patient in the hospital, and she loved testing the hardiness of the remote-controlled hospital bed!

Upon discharge, we gathered our stuff and walked out to the car. Suddenly, I felt a flood of memories pouring over me. It felt just like when we left the hospital on June 9, no longer pregnant, but without a baby. I burst into tears. As we tried to load into the car, some balloons tied to my backpack came loose. Constance joined me in my tears as the balloons floated away. I told Constance they were going up to Michael in heaven.

Constance missed two weeks of daycare and was on oxygen at night but eventually got better. Fortunately, I was between leaving my old job and officially starting Kinsman, so I had the time to spend with Constance—although it greatly tested my Type A personality. People were empathetic when they heard how sick she was, but that part felt trivial compared to the grief it triggered from losing Michael. People can relate to the stress of having a sick child, but most people cannot relate to the memories associated with a dead child. Of course, when I explained it, people were sympathetic, but having to explain it in order for people to empathize heightened my grief. It made me feel alone.

In the end, I was glad that I had the time to be with her and that, overall, she is a healthy little girl!

In the midst of Constance being hospitalized, it was open enrollment time for preschools, which was harder than I thought. We found a nice, three-day-a-week Christian preschool near our house. Even filling out the forms poked at my loss. Did Constance have a sibling? Yes, but is that really what they mean? Constance, in all her preciousness, often drew stick pictures of the four of us, so I listed Michael as her sibling. It felt relevant to include him.

Around this time, Cody came to live with us. According to Constance, Cody was a baby penguin chick. She told me he was her brother and would not get sick. For a few years, we did everything with Cody—pushed him on the swings at the playground, bought cookies for him at the grocery store, held his hand when we crossed the street, read stories to him at night. Even though I knew he wasn't real, I came to love him just as much as Constance did. Eventually Cody left our family. It was Constance's precious way of processing her own grief and desire for a sibling.

BIRTHDAY 2015

Shortly after Constance's hospitalization, my birthday came around again: February 21. The last two birthdays— my miscarriage with Daniel and finding out about Michael's health problems—were just about the worst ones anyone could imagine. I did not want to be around for it. I did not want to celebrate our usual way by going out to dinner with Brian, my parents, and Lynn and pretend to be happy. We explained to the parents that we were not doing a birthday celebration this year, and the three of us were going out of town.

We booked a weekend in the mountains and took off. As we drove out of town on Friday afternoon, a winter storm hit the mountains and the interstate was closed. Undeterred, we pulled over, regrouped at a bagel shop and made new reservations up in Boulder. We had a great time—swimming at the hotel, ice skating, and going out to eat. It was refreshing to break the pattern of the last two years. Just the three of us.

As winter slowly transformed into spring, I continued to work though my grief by reading my books and devotional, and rocking in Michael's room and looking at his pictures. I no longer needed to do it every night.

THE VIDEO

One Saturday in March, my brother-in-law called Brian. He wanted to let us know they were pregnant with their third child. He and his wife, my sister-in-law, wanted to know how to tell me, which was very thoughtful. Truthfully, there was no good way, and letting Brian break the news to me was best. It stung. Their oldest daughter was the same age as Constance. Now we had two miscarriages and a baby who died, and they were pregnant with baby number three.

We went to church the next day with that news hanging over our heads. Worship ended and the congregation settled into their seats. That particular Sunday, the associate pastor, Tim (with the pregnant wife, Michelle) gave the sermon. He introduced a video by stating that children are worth fighting for in this world. The sanctuary dimmed, and a young woman in a hospital bed appeared on the large screen overhead.

I felt my emotions go on high alert right away. *What was this video going to be about?* The video started with a husband

and wife explaining their birth story: "We were pregnant and went into labor early. Our baby's life was on the line." Suddenly, the nightmare of Michael's birth was playing out right before my eyes, in a very public, larger-than-life sort of way. I panicked, fighting back tears.

Like most church-going Christians, we default to sitting in the same seats every week. The problem in that moment was that our self-assigned spot was in the middle seat of the middle row of the sanctuary. I felt trapped. I was afraid to get up and make a scene. There was no way to leave without being noticed. Frozen, I just sat there. I looked down to avoid the images on the screen, but I couldn't drown out the audio. I felt like I was being bludgeoned with reminders of the most personal, inti- mate, worse moments of my life.

The woman's baby died in her arms, just like Michael. However, her story ended differently. She put the baby to her chest, and he started breathing again. It was a miracle. *Whoop- de-doo*. I wanted to leave, but the video ended and the house lights came back up. I was stuck. I sat through the sermon, no longer able to hold back the tears, and silently wept. Brian hugged me, and Lynn held my hand. They were crying too. Snot and tears flowed down my face as I tried not to make any noise while gasping for air.

The moment the last song started, I literally ran out of the sanctuary, pushing people out of my way. Brian sprinted to the children's area to get Constance. I just wanted to disappear. Charlotte found me and hugged me. I sobbed in her arms. Brian came back with Constance, and we ran to the car as people were starting to come out of the sanctuary. We didn't even buckle Constance in her car seat. We just drove away as fast as we could.

We decided to go out to lunch to debrief. We called Lynn since she had been sitting with us, and this was distressing for her too. She said that other women who knew us wept in the lobby. It was a very graphic, emotionally disturbing video. The images from it were similar to our Now I Lay Me Down to Sleep photos. Except the baby in the video didn't die. Pastor Joe called Brian right after church to see how we were doing. Tim called Brian later in the day to apologize, but I told Brian that was not good enough. I wanted an apology to my face, not through my husband or over the phone.

Now, although this was incredibly difficult, I also knew that Tim was a good, well-meaning person, and this was just a horrible oversight. I knew he did not realize how badly this would hurt us. After all, they joined the church right after we had Michael, so they didn't walk alongside us, as had so many other people at church. However, if you are going to preach at your home church, know your audience. I later found out that he added the video at the last minute, so Pastor Joe did not review it ahead of time either.

I was wrecked for the rest of the day and really for the rest of the week. My grief re-opened in full force. It stirred up emotions as powerful as when Michael was born. I fell back into a depression and realized that we weren't out of the woods yet—despite me wanting this experience to be "over." It just did not work that way, as much as I willed it to be.

I had just signed up for a ladies' Bible study at church that was starting that week. I did not feel like being around others, but I wanted to participate, so I made myself go. For some reason, after our losses, I have had a hard time being in groups of people, even with loving, Christian women whom I have known for a while. I was not going to let a traumatic Sunday keep me from my plans. But once I arrived, it was uncomfortable to be there. Anything that was brought up in discussion either seemed insignificant to me or related too closely to my grief. Mentally, I felt like I was on a completely different planet than the other ladies. I sat through the Bible study, fighting back tears.

In the end, we gathered in a circle for our closing prayer and prayer requests. I managed to get out five words, "I could use some prayer," before bursting into tears, unable to intelligibly utter anything further. But the women knew. They were at church on Sunday. They knew my struggle and surrounded me in a hug and prayer. I returned for one more study and stopped. I realized it was too difficult to be in a group setting.

We met with Tim and Michelle the next weekend. We each arranged to have a babysitter, and I appreciated their effort. I wanted to meet and clear the air. I did not want to hold a grudge. Truly, I wanted to heal from this in a healthy way, but I also wanted to acknowledge with them how significantly the video impacted us. Tim confessed he did not think about how the video would be received, he felt terrible, and he apologized. I appreciated that. We talked about how hard the loss had been for us, and that it didn't help that they were pregnant in addition to all that.

It was a good dinner. I didn't want to be BFFs with them, but it made it so we could look each other in the eye at church. Our current pastor teaches that as Christians, our church is our community. That doesn't mean we will always get along, but it does mean that we are called to love each other and forgive one another, just as Christ forgave us.

COUNSELING ... AGAIN

While we managed to make up with Tim and Michelle, my wound was still reopened by the event. On top of that, I was having flashbacks to the previous spring, remembering all the difficult parts we experienced carrying a terminal pregnancy. All the testing, the doctor appointments, and the bad news. Even the beautiful spring weather reminded me of our trial. At the time, I just did my best to get through it. But now that I had a year's perspective on it, I realized how traumatic the pregnancy itself was, aside from the birth.

String of Pearls had a counselor they usually recommended, but she had just retired. It seemed to take forever for them to find a new one. I looked for someone myself, but I was too nervous to make a decision. My previous counselor was great for self-identity issues but lackluster for grief and loss. Finally, Laura, the director of String of Pearls had a recommendation—Kim Wise, a counselor at Alternatives Pregnancy Center. Their office was across town, but it was worth it. String of Pearls even paid for the sessions, which was an incredible gift.

Brian and I did the counseling together. Like all counseling sessions, I started with my story of two miscarriages and a neonatal loss. Even though it felt like I was having a harder time than Brian, it was good to go together. Kim helped us see how to support each other while in different stages of grief and showed each of us that some comments we meant to be supportive were really detracting.

I did the last few sessions on my own. One of her most helpful insights was to push through the grief. I just wanted to get around it. Summarizing the words of Jerry Sittser from *A Grace Disguised*, Kim said the sun will rise more quickly if I am willing to walk through the darkness. Eventually there will be a sunrise.

On a lighter note, I told her I wanted another cat, but I knew it truly wouldn't replace my desire for a baby. She started to say, "Maybe a pet would …" I cut her off, however, and told her that we already had three. She quickly agreed another cat would not help!

MAY 2015

The counseling was good timing for the buildup to Michael's first birthday. I felt so sad in May—almost to the point of being non-functional—which surprised me. Like pretty much everything else, I wasn't expecting that. Constance's fourth birthday was May 15. I remembered planning her birthday the previous year—being pregnant with Michael and grateful for a fun distraction. This year was harder. I felt sad and not in the mood at all to plan a party. At least she was four and couldn't tell the difference between a Pinterest Party and a last-minute one. It had the basics—cake, games, and presents—and she loved it. I barely got an email invitation out two weeks before the event.

Immediately after Constance's birthday, the heaviness of Michael's birthday descended upon me. *What was happening to me?* I am normally an overly busy person who can't sit still. All I wanted to do was sit in the sunshine in my backyard and read my grief books and journal and cry. It was about all I was capable of doing. My geriatric care management business was just getting off the ground, and I was grateful that I was not too busy so I had time to sit and mourn.

FIRST BIRTHDAY

I dreaded going to church on Michael's birthday. His actual birthday was Monday, June 8, since it was on a Sunday the year before. But I strongly associated the day of the week with his birthday, in addition to the date. My first reaction was not to go to church at all. It would be too painful. *What if people said the wrong thing to me? Or even worse, what if they forgot completely?* I understood that the anniversary of our baby's birth and death was not as significant to others. But it was so important to me. I could not bear the thought of facing the friendly greeters when they inevitably said, "Good morning. How are you?" *I'm not fine. My baby died a year ago. Did you forget?*

But instead, we decided to embrace it. We asked Pastor Joe if we could share a bit during the church service. We invited our parents and my running friends. We put up a picture of me, Brian, and Michael on the overhead screen and shared what we learned in the last year—that God is always good, loving, gracious, and faithful, regardless of our circumstance. I shared how I learned about God's love in the midst of suffering and that He is the source of joy. And I thanked our congregation and friends for their support. It was wonderful. I am so glad that we asked for and were allowed the opportunity.

That evening we invited our parents over and watched the DVD of Michael's funeral. It was wonderful to view it again. Constance was able to understand that it was about baby Michael and was excited anytime she recognized one of us on the TV—especially herself! We went to bed satisfied with the day but also anticipating another hard one tomorrow.

JUNE 8, 2015

June 8. A day that will forever be precious to me. I took the recommendation from the psychiatrist and others to spend the morning remembering and grieving and the afternoon celebrating. I sat outside, of course, and did my grief ritual. I wrote in my journal:

Dear God, Good morning. I love you and worship you. Thank you for the sweet breeze. Today was the day Michael was born. Joy! Michael is one today. Joy! I made it a year. Joy! We had him and met him! Joy, joy, joy! But he is not here. He is not coming back. But yes, Lord, I will not forget. I will see him again! Now what? I will keep going on, like I did the day before. Lord, please be with me. In Jesus Name, Amen

I wrote a letter to Michael:

Dear Michael,

You would have been one today. You have been on my heart and mind every day since the day you were born. How can I grieve someone that I only knew for a day? But of course, I started to get to know you from the moment we found out about you. Michael, I miss you. I wish you were here. I can only picture you as a perfect, quiet, cuddly newborn. What are you like in heaven? Are you a baby in Jesus' arms? Are you a child running around? Are you a young man, strong and healthy? I know you are there and someday I will see you again! Love, Mom

It was such a powerful way to connect with him and to remember that he is a real person who existed on earth and now is in heaven. I always wonder what he is like and look forward to the day when I get to find out.

Brian had to work, which at first, I thought would be okay, but it really just sucked. I felt alone for much of our loss and here I was, alone again. I went out to lunch with my mom and then got a massage, which was nice. I held back my tears. The whole day was so tender. My emotions were fragile.

We received some calls, emails, cards, and texts. String of Pearls sent me a beautiful silver charm necklace. I was grateful for the people who remembered his birthday and acknowledged it.

Brian finally came home in the late afternoon, and we went to a small, local amusement park. By the time we left, traffic had started to build, and we got there late. Still, we had fun. As we pulled up to our house after a nice evening together, we saw our driveway had been anonymously covered in hearts with chalk. I later pieced together that it was a wonderful family from church who did something for us every year to mark Michael's birthday. Simple gestures such as these were exponentially touching to us.

We had birthday cake at home to cap off the day. It tasted like sawdust. It was our attempt to celebrate, but truly when you boil it down, a cake for a dead baby doesn't make it any better. By the time the evening came, I was ready for the day to be over and weary of holding my emotions together. Brian held me as I cried myself to sleep.

REFLECTIONS ON THE FIRST YEAR

I didn't expect having Michael would change my life so much. I thought it would be a one-time event, and then we would move on with our lives. As I reflected on the year, I realized Michael grew to have a real place in our family—we became a family of four. Just like having a living child, I think of Michael all the time, and we talk about him daily. I feel my love for him, and his presence in my life has grown more and more every day.

Having Michael also changed how I interact with the world around me. I now see things through the lens of surviving the death of my child. It gives me more compassion for those who are hurting but also puts the pettiness of so many other trials into perspective. In some ways, I am stronger. I can read stories about others who have lost children or loved ones. I read them with tenderness but not with the fear that others may feel who haven't experienced major loss. I used to think, *How could someone go through that?* Well, now I know. It's tough.

I understand why some people don't recover, but I also know that it is possible if you are willing to face the pain and work through it. In other ways, though, I still feel emotionally damaged. I am more sensitive to bad news and violence—regardless of whether it is a story about people I know personally, a national news story, or a movie. I have more or less stopped watching movies I haven't seen before. Whether happy or sad, violent or docile, they all seem to trigger a raw emotion in me.

Going though such a tough pregnancy and later dealing with the outcome gave me compassion and understanding for women who do choose to abort, although it doesn't change my understanding that it directly conflicts with God's design. Having now survived the death of our son makes me feel even more grateful that abortion wasn't an option we considered. But this was also the hardest experience in our life that we had gone through. We went through it as a married couple, with a wonderful partnership, a huge network of support with family and friends, a great church home, and good, stable incomes.

If our life was not on a firm foundation or if I didn't have a faith rooted in God, I could understand why choosing an abortion would seem like the easier route. Not pain-free, but easier. I'm grateful that this pregnancy opened my eyes to that reality. However, had we followed earthly reason, we wouldn't have escaped a difficult situation and, even more significantly, we would have missed the incomparable, irreplaceable opportunity to meet our son outside the womb. We would have missed the chance to touch him and to hold him before we handed him over to God. Brian would not have gotten to meet him at all, and Constance would not have even known about her brother. Michael was the blessing, the shining star in our horrible situation. Despite all the pain and grief, an abortion would have been a far worse option.

It is natural for humankind to try to avoid pain. We tend to seek the comforts and pleasures of this world. I learned that joy doesn't come from earthly comforts or happy circumstances. Pure, satisfying joy only comes from knowing the all-powerful and loving God who holds us in the palm of His hand. And nothing, not even death, can take that away.

Looking back, I now see that the first year was one of survival. I never expected it to be so hard. The pregnancy alone was such a hard thing unto itself—I thought our suffering would be over once Michael was born, even if he died. I had to work through the question: What does it mean to be a Christian in the midst of pain and suffering? It doesn't necessarily make it easier, but being a Christian gave me a framework to process the loss and hopefully start to heal in a healthy way. In my loss, I turned to God instead of away from Him. I brought my grief, my anger, and my questions to Him. Because when I didn't, I got stuck in my depression. There were times the first year when I felt like a survivor and times when I felt like I was barely holding on.

We included this verse in our Christmas card, and I reflected on it again at Michael's birthday: "We rejoice in hope of the glory of God. Not only this, but we also rejoice in our sufferings, knowing that suffering produces perseverance; and perseverance, proven character; and proven character, hope: and hope doesn't disappoint us, because God's love has been poured into our hearts through the Holy Spirit who was given to us" (Roman 5:2–5, WEB).

I see God's presence when I look back on the first year. King David writes: "The Lord is close to the brokenhearted and saves those who are crushed in spirit" (Psalm 34:18). I experienced that firsthand. I absolutely felt His blessing, His love, and His presence amidst our suffering. And I rejoice in that! As dark as some of our days were in the first year, God's light shined brighter. Looking back on what I gained, I wouldn't change our experience. We loved and carried Michael for seven months to get twenty minutes with him on earth.

It was absolutely worth it.

CHAPTER SEVEN

Jesse

SUMMER: BACK TO THE NEW NORMAL

It took a few days to recover after Michael's birthday, but by mid-June, I felt like a different person. A new person. I had survived the first year, and now that was behind us. Life did not feel so hard, and my emotions were not as delicate. My business was up and running. I had several clients and was contacted in the middle of June for my first big guardianship case. It is amazing to witness God's perfect timing firsthand.

Life went on. Brian was also busy expanding his business, so we did not take a vacation that summer. I kept running with my grief friends, and that was good. The summer ended, and Constance started preschool in the fall.

FALL: TRYING AGAIN

I view the year in two distinct parts. The first six months of the year are so tender, so full of hurt. Some women who have had losses talk about certain anniversaries—the date of their miscarriages, their due dates that never came, etc. For me, there are so many significant dates that they blend into a season. I associate the spring with miscarrying Daniel, carrying Michael, and grieving him in the buildup to his first birthday. The second half of the year is so much easier for me. His birthday has passed, and I survived. Of all our losses, the fall miscarriage with Sarah was easier and brought so much healing at the time, so while I remember her, it isn't as sad a time of year.

As much as I had done to process and accept the death of Michael, as well as the miscarriages with Daniel and Sarah, I still felt a hole in my life—Constance was almost four and a half, and I really wanted more children. The three of us had so much fun, but it didn't feel like our family was complete. Brian and I felt like we were ready to try again.

I made an appointment to talk to Dr. Ziernicki about it. The specialist at DRS said that having a baby with trisomy 18 does not predict that we would have a greater risk for another baby like that. I had already done some of the easier tests to rule out fertility problems such as an autoimmune disorder or a hormonal imbalance. Besides, I had carried a normal pregnancy. Brian and I were healthy, as was Constance. Dr. Ziernicki suggested we both have our karyotypes analyzed to make sure we did not have any weird chromosomal abnormalities. The test came back normal for both of us.

After praying about it, I felt ready to try again, which was so exciting! After two miscarriages and faithfully carrying a terminal pregnancy, I certainly hoped it would go differently! Surely, God would reward our faithfulness and bless us with another child. As Brian likes to say, we pulled the goalie from the net and went for it!

THE ADOPTION OPTION

We did not conceive in our first month of trying, and I was bitterly disappointed. I was very depressed the week I had proof that we weren't pregnant. Nevertheless, we were not deterred and continued to "try."

Around the same time, I started to feel God calling us to pursue adoption. It felt like every time I turned on the radio, surfed social media, or picked up a magazine, there was a story about adoption. My heart went out to the children. I even saw an advertisement for an adoption agency in a bathroom stall while at a funeral service! Brian and I had previously talked about adoption, but I always pictured being able to have our own biological kids first. I was sad that this was our option by default. I mustered up the strength to look into it.

It seemed like there were three options—domestic private adoption, adoption through the foster care system, or international adoption. After doing some web research, I found a Christian agency nearby. I nervously placed the call to RSVP for their next informational open house. The receptionist on the other end of the phone said their open house for November was full. I was instantly angered by it. *How could they be full?*

Didn't they know what a significant step this was for me to take? They put us on the waitlist and ended up having a couple spots open up after a snowy week.

We drove down to the meeting in Castle Rock, a town about forty-five minutes away. The moment we pulled into the parking lot, the thought hit me, *I don't want to go in.* The two-story building stood in front of me like a fortress. I didn't even want to get out of the car. Nevertheless, we did. After almost not being able to come due to a full registration, I expected to walk into a packed room. Instead, we sat around a conference table in a small room with four other couples. The seating arrangement made it impossible for me to blend in.

The director explained about their specific agency and about the adoption process in general. I learned that private, domestic adoption meant *babies.* In the United States, if something happens to an older child's parents, they go to the foster care system. So using a private agency for a domestic adoption means that you will be getting a baby (*and an EXPENSIVE one at that!*).

As a lovely lady went on and on and on about all the *wonderful* prenatal appointments and being able to attend the fairy-tale birth of your adopted child, I had flashbacks of all the horrible, horrible appointments that I had with Michael. There was no way I could attend those appointments with a young woman carrying our future baby. I never wanted to see another ultrasound again. I felt the tears welling up in me. I couldn't make eye contact with anyone, for if I did, the floodgates would open.

Brian saw I was having a hard time. I asked him to speak for us when it was our time to introduce ourselves and explain why we were interested in adoption. Whispering, I asked him not to look at me or even hold my hand. I put my walls up and stared at my lap. I just wanted to make it through the meeting.

Another woman who was there with her husband was practically jumping out of her seat like a teacher's pet. She asked all the questions and was ready to take a baby home with her that night. *You are so annoying. Please stop talking ...* I literally ran out of there immediately the moment it ended. I held in the tears until we left the parking lot so none of the other attendees would see. *Okay, I guess this isn't the type of adoption for us.*

PREGNANT!

A few weeks after the adoption agency's open house, we found out we were pregnant! Just as every pregnancy went, I was a few days late and anxiously peed on a stick. Since we were trying, and pretty good at conceiving by now, it was not a huge surprise. I was excited but guarded. This is what I wanted, but it felt bittersweet. My joy was overshadowed by pain and fear. We faithfully accepted our other miscarriages. We faithfully carried Michael. We loved him, held him, and gave him to the Lord. After all that, I was certain we would get a healthy child who would live.

Of course, all the innocence that those blissfully igno-rant first-time mothers had was long gone. I knew what could happen and just wanted the first trimester to be over. *Could someone just knock me out, and wake me up in twelve weeks?* I wanted to be one of those people who found out they were pregnant at twelve weeks, not five weeks or even four. *Who are those women? They might as well be unicorns.*

So now the wait began. I tried not to worry or think about it, which was not really possible. I didn't want to go to the doctor immediately, like we had the other times. I knew there was nothing good or bad they could tell me until at least eight weeks, so we waited until then. I took progesterone when I was pregnant with Michael. I always wondered if I would have miscarried if I did not take those pills. But would that have truly been a better outcome? Despite the heartache, I couldn't imagine my life without him or without experiencing that loss. This time, I did not want to rely on pills. I just wanted to see what would happen on its own.

Sharing the early news with our inner circle, however, was unexpectedly hard. *We are pregnant.* The words haunted me. I had said them so many times. But rather than bringing life, those words brought death. I felt depressed. We waited a week or two, and then I had Brian tell my parents. I couldn't even utter the words to my own mother. I didn't tell my best girlfriends.

Fortunately, around week six, I started feeling sick. Really sick! This is what I prayed for! I so desperately wanted to feel nauseated with Daniel and Sarah, just as I had with Constance. We were cautiously optimistic. This had to be a good sign.

PROJECT 1.27

Prior to finding out we were pregnant, we were planning to go to an overview night with another adoption organization called Project 1.27, a nonprofit that helps couples get certified to adopt through the foster care system. Even though we were pregnant now and would not try to adopt at the same time, I felt God leading us to go. This meeting, the first week of December, was a lot easier than the meeting at the private adoption agency, although parts were still difficult. I felt more prepared since we went to the other overview night the month before. Also, given the pregnancy, I felt like the pressure was off.

Some parents shared their experience of infertility and adopting. What I mostly remember is that the meeting room was above a butcher shop, and I was so nauseated from the wretched smells coming from below. While adopting out of the foster system sounded challenging, it seemed easier than going to prenatal appointments with a birth mom. We left with their information and put it on hold.

EIGHT-WEEK APPOINTMENT

December 10, 2015. It was finally time to see Dr. Ziernicki for our eight-week pregnancy confirmation appointment. I was nervous ... and nauseated! Brian had to pull over so I could throw up on the side of the road on our way there. *That has to be a good sign, right?*

We got to the doctor's office and were ushered into the ultrasound room. I had butterflies in my stomach the size of Pteranodons. So many bad memories were attached to our past ultrasounds. *It had to be different this time—it just had to!* The tech got started and fished around with her probe for the embryo as we all watched on the black-and-white computer screen.

She hesitated and said, "I'm having a hard time finding anything."

"Are you looking hard enough!?" I asked. "Look harder! Maybe to the side?"

The tears welled up. All our losses came flooding back. I knew. And predictably, I knew what was going to come out of her mouth next.

"Are you sure about your dates? Maybe you are off."

But I wasn't. Like all three times before. I was not off on my dates. I was never off.

She looked harder and said, "I'm sorry, there isn't anything there. I can't find a heartbeat. The gestational sac is there, but no fetus."

Tears poured down my face. Brian cried too. We sat together on the ultrasound table and hugged and sobbed. It was the most awful thing we could have heard at that moment. The tech told me to get dressed and that we could go directly to an exam room rather than back out to the lobby to wait for Dr. Ziernicki.

But I felt so sick! I had all the normal signs of pregnancy that I did not have with the miscarriages—breast tenderness, bloating, fatigue, nausea—I was not mistaken. The medical assistant came in and asked me all her stupid, routine questions. "Have you been nauseous?" "When was your last period?" I answered the questions as best I could. I could barely think coherently.

Dr. Ziernicki came in shortly after that. She immediately gave me a big hug, and I just wept. Handing me a box of tissues, she said she thought I had a blighted ovum and explained what that was. A fertilized egg attaches to the uterus, which signals to your body that you are pregnant, but for some reason it does not divide and turn into an embryo. She said we could wait a week to see if they missed something on the ultrasound and to give us time to decide what we wanted to do. I couldn't even think at all, so that sounded fine. She also checked my blood to see if my hormone levels were increasing.

Clutching the tissue box like a teddy bear, I cried so hard as we left the appointment. If I was not going to leave with news of a baby, then at least I was going to take the cheap, scratchy tissue box as a consolation prize. On the way out, I saw a different medical assistant who used to go to our church. I hadn't talked to her in a few years. I did not want to say hi, make pleasantries, or talk about our private situation. It was awkward. I was devastated. Although it wasn't certain yet, I could not believe we were going to miscarry again. We left the office in shock. It was finally time to tell some people that we were pregnant so they could pray and support us.

First, we called our parents. I still could not talk about it, so I emailed my best girlfriends, asking for prayer. It was difficult to even write the words. What a nightmare to ask for prayer and describe practically the same situation AGAIN.

The subject line of my email was "Not Again" and it was only four simple sentences:

Hi friends, I don't even know how to compose this stupid email. Our ultrasound today showed a blighted ovum. I have the hope/denial that they are wrong so we are repeating the ultrasound in a week. And I am totally nauseous which is the worst of both worlds. Love, Rosie

No pregnancy announcement, no explanation, no details. That is all I could get out. My friends were very supportive and sympathetic. They said they would pray, but that did not feel like enough. We shared with a few people at church, but we were not involved in a small group at the time and did not really know who to turn to.

Brian and I were able to spend the rest of the day together, which was great. After calling our parents, we went out to brunch and did a little Christmas shopping. It was actually nice. We nervously waited out the week and let Christmastime be a welcomed distraction.

I did, of course, Google "blighted ovum." What a terrible term. *My uterus is blighted, like an urban ghetto.* Sadly, because of this, there was not a heartbeat for our baby. I named the baby Jesse, although I was less certain if this little life "counted" without the heartbeat. *Whatever, it counts to me!* I didn't know if the baby would have been a boy or girl, but I felt like it was a boy, so that was what I went with. I also started loading up on the Zofran. Like with Michael, I wasn't going to feel nauseated for nothing!

A week passed and finally, it was the day of our second appointment. Same drill. Feel sick. Check into the doctor's office. Go into the crappy ultrasound room. The tech got started as we watched on the screen. No change at all. Definitely a miscarriage. I was just as upset as the week before, and we went back to the exam room.

A different medical assistant came in and started asking me the same dreadful questions as the week before. "How are you feeling?" "Are you nauseous?" *Yes.* "Describe your symptoms." I could barely talk.

Tearfully, I snapped at her, "I am going to miscarry! What does it matter?" She got defensive and said she was supposed to ask these questions.

I said, "I'm not going to answer any more questions. Just get my doctor." Brian handed me a tissue box and laid next to me on the exam table.

Dr. Ziernicki came in and gave me a hug.

"I snapped at your medical assistant."

"That's okay."

I told her I just wanted to do the D&C. It was Friday, December 18. I did not want to do it before Christmas. *Let's not have Christmas be TOTALLY ruined.* Dr. Ziernicki said she could do it Saturday, December 26. *Still too close.* We agreed on Tuesday, December 29. I figured that would be a good week because work would be slow, and I could easily take time off to recover. We made it through a dismal Christmas, overshadowed by our loss. At least we had already simplified it from the year before, which helped.

Dr. Ziernicki had switched practices between having Michael and this miscarriage. The new office didn't have a special room to do procedures, so we had to do the D&C at the hospital. And since it was at the hospital, I would have to go under general anesthesia. Interesting, because of that mere change, it increased the cost of the procedure ten times! Healthcare costs are ridiculous, and I am sure we can all agree on that.

Dr. Ziernicki recommended that I take Cytotec pills orally to soften my cervix the night before to make the procedure easier. Those were the same pills I took vaginally (*yuck*) to induce the very first miscarriage with Daniel. I took them around 9:00 p.m., right before we went to sleep. I worried that the pills would start the miscarriage before I got to the hospital on Tuesday morning.

Around 3:00 a.m., I woke up with horrible cramping, diarrhea, and bleeding. I felt awful. I was scared that the miscarriage was starting and so I lay there awake, afraid to move. We had to be at the hospital at 5:30 a.m., but when our alarm went off, I was already starting to bleed, so I told Brian I wanted to get there as soon as possible. I just wanted this horrible thing to be over with.

We got to the hospital and checked in for surgery. Even though this was my third D&C, it felt like a bigger deal since we were on the outpatient surgery floor at the hospital rather than at my OB-GYN clinic. I softly cried as we got checked in. The nurses, like always, were so nice and compassionate. Dr. Ziernicki arrived, and I said goodbye to Brian as they prepared me for the procedure. They wheeled me down the hall and into the operating room. It was freezing. They put me on the table, under the bright surgical lights. I tried hard to stay awake, because I always worry that the doctor will think I am knocked out when I am still able to feel things. That, of course, was the last thing I remember.

Next thing I knew, they were trying to wake me up. I always get severe shivers after surgery, and they had to give me more medication of some sort. Then Brian was allowed to come see me. It was over. Our fifth pregnancy was officially done. My heart broke. Again.

Brian took me home, and I went up to my bed. I was actually surprised how well I felt physically. I was so groggy after the other two D&Cs, but this time, with general anesthesia, I felt okay. I still stayed in bed all day, and Brian and I played a few board games together.

I gave myself a week to mourn the miscarriage. I thought, *I can control this.* I knew it would take time. A week was the amount of time I was willing to allot to the problem. I thought that since I had been through two other miscarriages, I knew how to handle it. I also thought that since I survived losing a child, a miscarriage should be no big deal. *Ugh! When am I ever going to learn?* Grief doesn't operate on my own timeline, and these losses are significant!

A NEW YEAR: GRIEVING JESSE

I was so happy for the new year to begin and for the holiday season to be over. I wanted to go back to work and back to a normal routine. I got two new clients right after the start of the new year and happily dove into work, pretending that everything was "fine." But in reality, I was not okay. I felt unspeakably sad, yet I dismissed it in my mind and tried to ignore it. I felt so sad, just as I had so many times now. I did not have any new words to explain how I felt.

After Michael died, I gathered up the pieces of my heart and put them back together. Not only was my heart ripped out from me again, but it was now shattered. Like old roadkill on the highway, being crushed over and over again.

I had a hard time talking about it. I couldn't put the depth of my emotions into words. "Sad" didn't even touch the magnitude of despair that I felt. I pictured an abyss of unending sorrow.

As I tried to move on, I encountered people who either knowingly or innocently asked, "How are you?" I said I was fine. What else could I say? *I had ANOTHER miscarriage. I am sad AGAIN.* I was afraid people would say, "There goes Rosie, the sad person. The one who is always going through a loss." I felt so foolish that we tried again without doing more testing. As the quote by Albert Einstein goes, insanity is doing the same thing over and over again but expecting a different outcome. *Eventually, conception would lead to life, right?* It does for so many other people. But not for us.

Within days of our miscarriage, I said to Brian, "Let's move forward with adoption." We printed out the registration forms for Project 1.27 and started filling them out. It was a disaster. I could not even fill out the first form without crying, so we quickly decided to put adoption on hold again.

I was having a hard time coping at work since I was not mentally healed. The world of senior care is turbulent. My clients are complex, and their families are often volatile. People need a care manager to sort through the chaos and dysfunction. But I was not standing on solid ground myself. I was uncertain and anxious. So when the normal problems with my frail clients arose, they sent me into ever-greater despair.

Around February, I finally admitted to myself that this miscarriage was significant. Despite going through it twice before (or perhaps because of it), it was even harder this time. Even though the miscarriage was not the same as losing Michael, parts of it were just as heart-wrenching.

Once I realized that this loss was significant, I tried to bring it before the Lord. Here is my journal entry from Valentine's Day, 2016:

A fourth loss. A fourth pregnancy without a child in my arms. A fourth round of grief. God, I am so sad. I can't handle anything. Lord, I'm sorry for my life! I'm sorry I'm failing. I hate what my life has become. God, I'm sorry I put myself into my work rather than coming to you. For how much I want a second child. I am embarrassed that I am grieving again. People are going to say there is Rosie—always sad. Not doing the things she should be at home, work, or church. Where is the misfits club? I had a miscarriage. I tried to brush it under the table and I am falling apart. I tried to escape into work and now that is a disaster. Dear Lord, I am so lost. I let it go to You.

This loss impacted me in a different way than the others. It felt so painful. Two miscarriages—that's heartbreaking, but it happens. Losing a baby—rough. *But now four losses in a row!?* It just felt like too much to bear. I searched the internet for blogs or chatrooms with other moms in my situation. I found people who had neonatal deaths and people who had multiple miscarriages, but I had a hard time finding people who had gone through both. I knew I was not the only one, but I could not find a lot of stories that I could relate to. And although miscarriages are so common, I only had one good girlfriend who had multiple miscarriages.

Even harder than admitting the significance of the loss was making sense of it theologically. Through all the other losses, I trusted God. I knew He was with me. I knew He was good and had a plan. I knew He loved me. I grieved the first two miscarriages with Him. I relied on Him as I carried Michael and as I mourned him after he was born.

But again? God?! How could this happen to me? Just as my heart was shattered, my faith was shattered too. One Sunday in church, the worship pastor led us through the song, "It Is Well With My Soul." I couldn't sing those words. It wasn't well with my soul! My soul was awful. Death still had its sting. I thought since we had trusted in Him through our other losses, He would bless us with a baby.

Throughout all of this, I wrestled with the false premise that if God loves us, He will bless us with children. Everything I knew in my head about God, I no longer felt in my heart. However, I knew truth doesn't change, so I continued to pursue understanding our situation within the context of my Christian faith. It took discipline.

My birthday came and went. It was the three-year anniversary of our first miscarriage and the two-year anniversary of finding out about Michael. I did not want to escape to the mountains like last year, but it was still a painful day. I opted to go out to brunch with my family, rather than dinner. I knew that by the evening, I would just be sick of it all.

I could not process my grief. I felt like I had been there so many times before. I decided to go back to counseling. I called Kim Wise, the grief counselor that Brian and I had seen the year before, and I left her a message. Another spring and another round of counseling. About a week after contacting her, I received an email back from Kim. She wrote, "I am truly sorry to hear about your loss but I am on maternity leave. Here are some recommendations for other counselors." *What? #&^\$#%&!! My neonatal loss counselor is on maternity leave?!* I could see the irony in this, but it also felt like I was being kicked when I was down.

I picked one of her recommendations and made the call. Another counselor. Another person to tell my now very long story to, just to get her caught up to speed. She was young. She was nice. She seemed pretty new at counseling, but she got the job done. I just needed someone to talk to so I would be able to put words behind my feelings.

She gave me a book to read about another woman who had a neonatal death. She cautioned that it was not quite the same ending as mine. I read the book. Parts were helpful. I always like hearing other people's stories. I got to the end of her story about faithfully carrying, mourning, and losing her son, just like Michael ...

… And now she was pregnant. She wrote, "I put my trust and hope in God. He kept his promise and gave us the gift of another life inside me."

OMG! I simultaneously wanted to barf and drop kick the book across the universe. *That is the ending of the book!? Her baby died and now God is blessing her by having another one?!* I HATED her ending. Why wasn't it my ending?! What about when things don't work out? Is God any less there for me? I knew the answer was no, but it was maddening to read it.

My anxiety continued to grow. I began having massive panic attacks. After feeling like I was having a heart attack one weekend, I called up my psychiatrist, Dr. Norwood, for some medication. This time, she gave me a prescription for an anti-depressant and anti-anxiety medication. She was incredibly affirming about the significance of loss upon loss. The medication helped ground my thoughts. It allowed me to breathe and feel like I could cope with our loss.

Processing my feelings about our miscarriage and the sum of our losses bled into the buildup to Michael's second birthday. I was not expecting to feel this sad two years after his birth. With my business in full swing, I realized this was the first year that I was attempting to do normal life and cope with his anniversary at the same time. Last year, I was just getting my footing underneath me. I did not have a full caseload and had time to grieve. This year, life was busy.

After our miscarriage in January, I had the urge to go on vacation. We did not go on vacation the previous summer, and taking an annual family vacation, just the three of us, was not part of our routine. Sure, we travel a lot, but it is usually to visit relatives, which is different. I nervously brought it up to Brian that I felt like we needed to go somewhere and have some fun over the summer. Brian agreed, and we booked a trip to Puerto Vallarta for the end of May, right after Constance's preschool classes ended for the summer but before Michael's birthday.

I was a total basket case as I tried to get ready for the trip. But once we left, it was amazing. We flew down to Puerto Vallarta and took a hotel shuttle to our resort. I instantly felt lighter the moment I stepped off the bus and into paradise—it was as if I shed the scales of grief. It felt so good to be at the beach in a beautiful location. I hadn't realized how empty I was and how badly I needed some R&R. We had a great trip, and I felt like a completely different person after we returned. I had never had a vacation deliver such a positive psychological impact.

We returned from vacation a few days before Michael's birthday. It was still a tender, wearisome day. We had a similar celebration as the year before, with time to reflect, eat some cake that still tasted like sawdust, and have some family fun. This year, Brian wanted to include our parents, since it was their grandson too. I hated that. I did not want to be around anyone else, even our parents.

Later, another counselor I saw gave me some good advice about how to approach Michael's birthday. First, he asked, "Do you enjoy having the cake?"

"No, it's painful."

"Yeah, it seems weird to put two candles on a cake for someone who did not live." Trying to do actions that don't match the emotions can make the day even harder. He also said if we did not want our parents around, that is okay. He clarified that losing our son does not equate to them losing their grandchild. They did not spend time doing grandparent things. They can be sad because of our loss, but it's not theirs.

That made a lot of sense to me. As with all of this, I have learned through experience what works for us and what does not. I hope that others can learn from our experience too, although I understand what works for me may not for someone else.

YEAR THREE

After Michael's second birthday passed, I thought, *I made it. Again. I survived the first two years after losing Michael.* The next year, Year Three, had its ups and downs but was generally better than Year Two. There were still some challenging moments. Unexpected triggers seemed to come out of nowhere. But they were fewer and fewer, and life felt more like that "new normal" that I had previously hated people telling me about. During Year Three, I worked, I spent time with my precious family, and I was content with the "new normal," as I proudly wore my cross necklace with Michael's ashes.

Christmastime and the anniversary of our last miscarriage was unexpectedly hard—*geez have I STILL not learned anything?* The incongruity between how I felt and the presumed joy of the holiday season was poignant. I grieved the loss and did not feel hopeful about the new year.

We tried to restart the adoption process in January, and I couldn't handle it—again. It triggered such a major grief reaction that led me to go back to counseling to continue to work out the big "Why?" *Why can't we have more kids? Why is this so hard? Why hasn't God answered my prayer?*

I resisted going back to counseling. Brian reminded me that grief is not linear. After all I have learned, I still want it to be! I still want to ignore it and hope it will just go away on its own. But it won't. This time the counselor was very reassuring, "You are just coming out of the white water now. You haven't had a calendar year without a loss in four years."

We decided to stop pursuing adoption and pregnancy. I finally surrendered as completely as I knew how, and I was overcome with a feeling of relief. It felt good. It felt right. After four years, I finally let go and was content to just be still before the Lord. Our string of losses was over. I was free and at peace to just be. We went on with our life, enjoying the normal rhythms of our little family.

CHAPTER EIGHT

The End?

I WOULD LOVE TO END THIS STORY with the news that we are pregnant. Wouldn't that make a great ending? That's not real life in this case. We are neither pregnant nor have we adopted a child. I don't know what God has planned for us. I don't know why we went through this.

That's not really how you are supposed to end a book—at least not according to my high school English teachers. We want a satisfying resolution. But what I do know is that I am here. I am okay. And that in itself is incredible. Though the losses were incredibly difficult, I have peace and acceptance about what happened.

Our fourth loss really triggered those big "Why?" questions, which took over a full year to work out. *Why did this happen to me? Why couldn't these losses have been avoided altogether?* What I learned is that God doesn't necessarily have to tell me why. He is sovereign and good, all the time, but we live in a fallen world. When Adam and Eve sinned, death entered into God's creation and perverted it down to our very cells. Nothing is immune to the fallen nature of this world— from natural disasters to miscarriages to death. Infertility, miscarriages, and the pain of neonatal death were not part of God's original plan.

To expect God to give an answer to "Why me?" is a false expectation. I am subject to this world's indiscriminate hardships just as much as anyone else. We feel God owes us an answer. He doesn't owe us that at all. Suffering is not always going to make sense or have a reason behind it. Despite our four years of suffering, I know that God is good. God is faithful. God is love. When one loses his or her focus on those truths, things start to fall apart. I have come to accept that I may not get an answer to "Why me?" on this side of heaven.

CHURCH—FOR BETTER OR WORSE

Attending church throughout the time of our losses played a key role in working through my grief. Encountering God every Sunday morning was sweet. As I sat in the sanctuary, listening to people worship, I was able to tenderly connect with God. Often, I was too tearful to sing out loud, but I followed along in my heart. I would just sit there and cry with my head on Brian's shoulder. It was nice. And exhausting.

Being part of a faith community was instrumental to receiving the support that we needed, yet it came with its own challenges, because churches, like any group environment, are made up of imperfect individuals. Sometimes people want to equate church with God, which leads to a distorted perspective of who God is. God is perfect. People, who make up the church, are not. Yet without people, the church wouldn't exist.

In many ways, I felt wonderfully supported and lifted up by the church leadership while we were pregnant. Along with the other congregants, they prayed for us, asked us how we were doing, and walked alongside us. The elders came over and prayed for us several times leading up to Michael's birth.

In other ways, the support we received fell short. While we were pregnant, we were the interim leaders of the children's ministry. The irony didn't go unnoticed that we were planning Sunday school for others while we were carrying a very sick baby that might never be a recipient of the ministry. I wish someone at church had said to me, "Roseanne, there is a time for everything. Now is not the time to volunteer!" But no one did. We served until Michael was born, which effectively was our resignation from children's ministry.

I wish someone on the leadership was able to recognize that it wasn't healthy to lead a ministry during that time when I wasn't wise enough to realize it myself. After having Michael, I felt guilty for not stepping back into volunteering. Now I look back, with a better understanding of the magnitude of our loss, and I can see how ridiculous that is. But at the time, I just felt guilty. Why didn't anyone tell me it was okay not to do anything?

At first, right after Michael was born, we were overwhelmed with support. The funeral service was beautiful. Individual church members were vital to holding us up during the hardest times. So many people came to Michael's funeral, brought us meals, and continued to pray for us. One dear woman went grocery shopping for me every week for a few months!

But a few months after Michael was born, I felt the support drop off from the church leaders even though that was when I needed the encouragement even more. Over the next two years, I often felt our loss was forgotten by those who planned the church services. About five other women in our small church got pregnant pretty soon after we had Michael. Week after week, the leaders seemed to joyfully announce from the pulpit that there was going to be a baby boom in the nursery and more volunteers were needed.

I didn't expect the church to stop operating under "business as usual," but it would have been nice if someone thought, "How is this announcement going to affect a newly grieving mother?" Time after time, there were incidents on Sunday mornings that pushed on my pain. We would be sitting in church and be broadsided with a birth announcement. Or have a baby dedication that morning without notice. And, of course, there was "the video."

It would have been really helpful for someone to have been my spiritual grief guide at church. To ask, "How can we be sensitive to a grieving member in our church?" But no one did. In hindsight, we could have told someone how hard it was, but as the grieving person, I was unable to identify it at the time.

There were times over the first two years that we considered leaving our church. I can understand why people do leave after major losses. Encountering others while I was grieving was hard. It was just too hurtful to feel forgotten by people who, from my perspective, "should have known."

On what would have been Michael's second Christmas, I was asked to skip the Christmas Eve service and help out in the nursery. I told the new children's ministry leader that I still walked the long way around the church so I didn't even go past the nursery, let alone enter it! I told him the last baby I held was a dead one. He got the point.

Of all the feelings that I have had to work through, letting go of my hurts from the church has taken the longest. A few years later, I now feel better on most Sundays. Now I am happily serving in different ministries. But I still have hard mornings at church. I anticipate that if something might be challenging at church, I just skip it. I skip days when they may announce a new birth or have a baby dedication. I put no pressure or obligations on myself for May and June. And Mother's Day? Forget it!

Collectively, our church isn't perfect. But despite our church's shortcomings, the blessings outweigh them. We continue to feel very loved by our individual friends and even the leaders who weren't aware of the ways that made our pain harder at times. Overall, it is better to be part of an imperfect church body, with its blessings and opportunities for grace, than to not be a part of a faith community at all.

ACCEPTANCE

Things still trigger my grief. One day, I may be happy to hear about a friend's successful pregnancy or be able to look at someone's baby pictures, but another day, it may send me into jealous despair. It was not until three years after Michael died that I was genuinely happy for a friend who became pregnant. And it was such a good feeling! I was happy that I was happy! But there are still times that I feel spitefully angry when I hear someone else's joyful announcement. I am sorry that my reactions to others' pregnancies aren't consistently positive, but they just aren't.

The desire to expand our family is still an unresolved issue in our lives. When I press into my desire, there is still some pain. I want another child. I don't know if it's in God's will. I don't know if we should try biologically again or try to adopt. Or if we should just do nothing. I can't imagine getting pregnant again, but I don't want to give up either. The future is unknown, but I put my trust in Him. God is bigger than this situation and far greater than what I can see or understand.

As more time passes, I can separate myself from our experience and see how it has changed me. I am able to draw great strength from looking back at all we went through and know that I have more than just survived. I am such a stronger person, like a sword that has been tempered in the fire. And while I wish no one would experience infertility, a miscarriage, or neonatal death, I don't regret that it happened to me. I accept it and am okay with what we have experienced. In the context of living in a fallen world, I wouldn't change what has happened.

Through these series of losses, I have gained so much! I have met so many other women who are mourning losses just like I am mourning. I have received encouragement from them and also been in a position to empathize with those who are still grieving. I have greater compassion for those who are going through similar losses and even seemingly unrelated hardships, like facing chronic debilitating diseases or other deaths.

As time goes by, I look at my losses differently. There are so many aspects to each loss, and time gives me a chance to work on each little part as it surfaces. Michael's death feels different to me one month out, one year out, and three years out. Just as God calls us to "work out your salvation with fear and trembling" (Philippians 2:12), my grief is still being worked out. My healing is continually evolving. A wise leader in my church once told me, "When it is all said and done, it isn't the pain that matters. It's the healing." I think about Michael and our experience with a feeling of peace and even joy.

I wrestled with the fact that God did not heal me any of the times that we asked Him to. None of my pregnancies were miraculously saved. However, we learned that God works in these experiences for His glory—whether He chooses to heal us or not. In the end, this experience—even without a miracle—has left us with a testimony about God's goodness, mercy, and love. It would be easy enough to praise God for answering our prayer for healing. I believe our testimony is actually more powerful and can be used to help more people because we were not healed. I praise God regardless of the outcome and despite our losses! I praise God for Michael's life. I praise God that Michael is our son and that we got to meet him. Death doesn't change that fact!

Some people said God will bless us for our faithfulness. In our pain, that was hard to hear. At the time, I thought, *What blessing? I am miserable.* I couldn't see any good in our situation. But I was willing to extend a mustard seed measure of trust and walk the path set before us. Our perspective on earth is so limited. Our understanding of time is limited. I know others have been impacted by what we have gone through.

I know I have children in heaven, and I can't wait to see them! My heart yearns for when we will be reunited in heaven and I will meet Daniel, Sarah, and Jesse and get to spend more than twenty minutes with Michael.

And with that thought, I praise God! Alleluia, all glory and praise be to Him!

Appendix

Dear Reader,

Thank you for reading my story! If you have experienced a similar loss: First of all, I am so sorry. You are now in the club that no one wants to be in. And second, I encourage you to write out your feelings. Write what happened. Write to God. Write to your baby. I hope this helps. You are not alone.

At first, I decided to write down my story so that I could remember what happened and when. Parts of it were starting to blur together, and I did not want to forget. In doing so, I found that it was very healing in that it led me to process parts of the losses that I hadn't worked through yet.

I also wrote it to share with others not only what I have been through, but more importantly, to give hope, encouragement, and support to other women who, unfortunately, are going through something similar. I hope this book will also help professionals who work with women who have experienced pregnancy loss.

Finally, I wanted to honestly share how my faith in God was both a source of support and a struggle at different times of my experience. It is possible to rely on God and yet wrestle with the loss at the same time. If you read this book and want to find out more about who God is and how He cares for YOU, please email mychildreninheaven@gmail.com. I will send you a Bible and find a local connection to a believer wherever you live.

"Are not two sparrows sold for a penny? Yet not one of them will fall to the ground outside your Father's care. And even the very hairs of your head are all numbered. So don't be afraid; you are worth more than many sparrows" (Matthew 10:29–31).

My relationship with God is the most important thing in my life. Without God, nothing else matters—not my spouse, not my daughter, not my losses. God is real and wants to know you too.

I believe we live in a fallen world and fall short of being perfect. In our imperfection, we sin, which means doing something against the goodness and nature of God. Jesus paid the price for our sin by giving his life. All it takes is saying this prayer, either words in your mind or out loud to God: "God, I want to know You. I have sinned. I give my life to You and acknowledge that Jesus died on the cross for me. Please come into my life. Amen."

Again, thank you for reading my story and I hope it is an encouragement to YOU!

With love, Roseanne Collison

Mom to Constance, Michael, Daniel, Sarah, and Jesse

All for You, Michael

We found out about you and ...
I took vitamins for you.
I felt sick for you.
I wore big clothes for you.
I gained weight for you.
I ate whatever I could get down for you.
I prayed for you.
I longed for you.
I ached all over for you.
I felt you.
I loved you from the moment I knew you.
You were a part of me.

We told people about you.
We talked to you.
We sang to you.
We rubbed you.
We prayed for you.
We waited for you.
We wanted you.

But then …
We lost you.
We held you.
We cried for you.
We grieved you.
We couldn't stop thinking of you.
We made memories of you.
We prayed for you.
We could do nothing to stop you from leaving us.
We gave you to Jesus.
We promised you that we would see you again.
You are with your Father in heaven, but we are your parents now and forever more. We think about all the things that we did for you and we would do it all over again, just to know you.

Love, Your Mom and Dad

Based on the poem by Erin McSparron, *Teardrop Diary*.
Rearranged by Roseanne Collison. Used with permission.

Recommended Reading and Resources

RECOMMENDED READING

Audrey Bunny, Angie Smith, B&H Publishing Group, 2013.

Empty Cradle, Broken Heart, Deborah L. Davis, Fulcrum Publishing, 1996.

Experiencing Grief, H. Norman Wright, B&H Publishing Group, 2004.

A Gift of Time, Amy Kuebelbeck and Deborah L. Davis, Johns Hopkins University Press, 2011.

A Grace Disguised, Jerry Sittser, Grand Rapids,

MI: Zondervan Publishing, 1996.

Heaven is For Real, Todd Burpo and Lynn Vincent, Thomas Nelson Publishing, 2010.

Holding On to Hope, Nancy Guthrie, Tyndale House Publishers, 2002.

I Will Carry You, Angie Smith, B&H Publishing Group, 2010.

Teardrop Diary, Erin McSparron, LuLu Publishing, 2005.

The One Year Book of Hope, Nancy Guthrie, Tyndale House Publishers, 2005.

We Were Gonna Have a Baby, But We Had an Angel Instead, Pat Schwiebert, Grief Watch, 2003.

WEBSITES
String of Pearls, www.stringofpearlsonline.org

Alternative Pregnancy Center, www.youhavealtermatives.org

Now I Lay Me Down to Sleep, www.nilmdts.org

If you would like Roseanne to speak to your group about faith, maternity losses, or overcoming grief, please email mychildreninheaven@gmail.com.

Made in the USA
Columbia, SC
24 June 2021